WALES BEFORE 1066
—A GUIDE

DONALD GREGORY

WALES
BEFORE 1066
— A GUIDE

by

DONALD GREGORY

First edition: 1989
Reprinted: May 1992
Revised edition: 2008
© Text: Donald Gregory

ISBN: 978-1-84524-096-7

Maps by Ken Gruffydd

Cover Design: Sian Parri

First published in 1989 by Gwasg Carreg Gwalch
12 Iard yr Orsaf, Llanrwst, Wales LL26 0EH
☎ 01492 642031 📠 01492 641502
✆ books@carreg-gwalch.com
Web site: www.carreg-gwalch.com

Revised edition published in 2008 by Llygad Gwalch,
Ysgubor Plas, Llwyndyrys, Pwllheli, Gwynedd LL53 6NG
☎ 01758 750432 📠 01758 750438
✆ books@carreg-gwalch.com
Web site: www.carreg-gwalch.com

To my wife, Helen who has been exploring Wales with me for forty years.

By the same author:
"Yesterday in Village Church and Churchyard"

LIST OF MAPS AND ILLUSTRATIONS
MAPS

ILLUSTRATIONS

CONTENTS

INTRODUCTION

In 1536 the Act of Union was heralded in London as the union of England and Wales, whereby the two countries were to become one, the age-old differences in race, culture and history expected miraculously to fuse together in the parliamentary crucible. Four hundred and fifty years later however these differences remain, despite the widespread intermarriage of the two races and despite the almost complete interdependence of the two countries brought about by the technological marvels of modern communications.

To many English people the real history of England began with the Norman conquest; all that went before is regarded as an interesting collection of stories about prehistoric man, the Celts and the Romans, the Saxons and the Danes, which together provide a picturesque introduction to the main narrative. The people of Wales on the other hand tend not to look at their past in this way at all; to start with, very many Welshmen have ancestors who lived in Britain long before the arrival in these islands of the forebears of most contemporary English people. It has to be remembered too that the Welsh have not always been mostly confined to the hills in the west: circumstances, as will be shown, drove them further and further back into the hills until some sort of a line of demarcation between Wales and England was established in the eighth century by the Mercian king, Offa.

Early settlers in these islands though the Welsh were, they were by no means the first to live in what we now call Wales. Something will be said of their predecessors when the prehistory of the country is under consideration. Suffice it to say here that the Celts, who were the ancestors of those who today live in Ireland, in the Highlands of Scotland, in Brittany and in Wales, crossed the Channel into these islands in about 500 BC, their arrival being thought to mark the end of the Bronze and the beginning of the Iron Age. When five hundred years later, in the first century A.D. the Romans invaded Britain, they found that these Celts were firmly established in the hilly country in the west, where, roused by their Druidical religious leaders, with whom the Romans had already clashed in Gaul, they presented a fierce challenge to the invaders. The animated crowds of Rugby supporters who every other year cross the Dee, the Severn and the Wye to shout encouragement to their fellow countrymen at Twickenham, are the proud representatives of a sturdily independent, unassimilated and radically different racial group from the English.

In this book the story of Wales before 1066 has been divided into four chronological parts, each being immediately followed by an account of what may still be seen to illustrate the separate historical surveys.

PREHISTORIC WALES

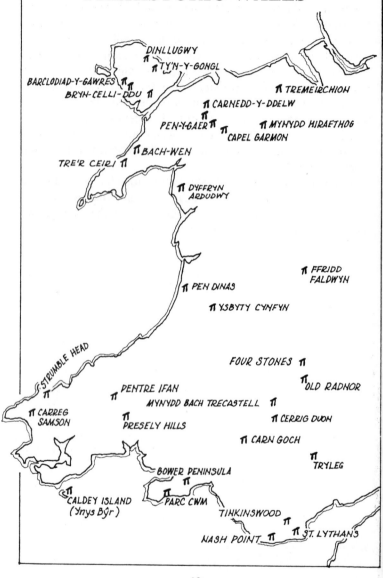

DINLLUGWY
TY'N-Y-GONGL
BARCLODIAD-Y-GAWRES
BRYN-CELLI-DDU
TREMEIRCHION
CARNEDD-Y-DDELW
PEN-Y-GAER
MYNYDD HIRAETHOG
CAPEL GARMON
BACH-WEN
TRE'R CEIRI
DYFFRYN ARDUDWY
FFRIDD FALDWYN
PEN DINAS
YSBYTY CYNFYN
STRUMBLE HEAD
FOUR STONES
OLD RADNOR
PENTRE IFAN
MYNYDD BACH TRECASTELL
CARREG SAMSON
CERRIG DUON
PRESELY HILLS
CARN GOCH
TRYLEG
BOWER PENINSULA
CALDEY ISLAND
(Ynys Bŷr)
PARC CWM
TINKINSWOOD
NASH POINT
ST. LYTHANS

PREHISTORIC TIMES

A. GENERAL SURVEY

The earliest inhabitants

Northern Europe in its prehistory was several times covered with vast sheets of ice; in the intervals between these ice ages there were long interglacial periods, when life abounded. Enough evidence has accumulated in recent years to prove that early men sometimes took shelter during these interglacial periods in the limestone caves to be found in the Clwyd valley. No skeleton has survived but enough human bones have come to light to enable archaeologists to determine, thanks to the wonders of radio carbon dating methods, just when the human occupation of these caves took place. The date agreed is c. 180,000 B.C. The ice subsequently returned and human life disappeared from the valley only to return once again when the next interglacial period made human occupation possible in other limestone caves in the same valley. This later occupation has been carbon-dated as c. 50,000 B.C.

In the last ice age which ended somewhere between 10,000 and 9000 B.C., ice covered the whole of Wales except for the most southerly part of Dyfed and the Gower Peninsula in Glamorgan, where in a cave in the parish of Paviland in the south-west corner of the peninsula, south-east of Worms Head, an early archaeologist from Oxford, William Buckland, in 1823 discovered a human skeleton which had been buried along with ivory implements and the bones of a mammoth. Some ritual was believed to have accompanied the interment, as the skeleton, which was found in a standing position against the wall of the cave, was stained red. The excited Dean had the precious find taken to Oxford, where it acquired the interesting name of The Red Lady of Paviland. Archaeologists today have more sophisticated tools at their disposal; in consequence it is now known that the skeleton, which had been stained red by the iron oxide in the soil, was of a young man of about twenty-five years of age. Furthermore carbon dating proved that the young man died in about 16,500 B.C., some ten thousand years after the death of the mammoth found with him.

In later excavations archaeologists found signs of human activity in other caves in Wales, but only in the Gower Peninsula has a skeleton been found. The young man of Paviland died seven and a half thousand years before the ice started to melt, the representative to posterity of the Palaeolithic or Old Stone Age. In the difficult centuries of transition that followed the very gradual withdrawal of the ice, groups of hunters roamed the shores and hills of Wales, using small flint tools to ensure an adequate supply of food, both fish and animal. Some of these Mesolithic or Middle Stone Age microliths have been found, especially in the south-west of Wales. Some time after 6000 B.C. the level of the sea, which had become swollen as the ice melted, had risen sufficiently for the land bridge with the continent to be broken, thus separating Britain from the mainland of Europe.

Neolithic Wales

"The Stone Age, the Bronze Age, the early Iron Age pass through the Welsh memory like a blurred dream...all over Wales they have their monuments; crumbled stone villages and turf-covered forts...burial chambers, cromlechs, and most haunting of all, the single enigmatic boulders which stand here and there all alone in empty landscapes, as markers, as memorials or perhaps as warnings." Jan Morris, *The Matter of Wales*. The forebears of those who brought the ideas that were to constitute the neolithic revolution in Wales hailed from the three great river valleys of the Middle East, the Nile, the Tigris and the Euphrates. Remarkable changes that occurred in those parts between 6000 and 5000 B.C. gave rise to a revolution in the pattern of living that probably had no equal in significance in the story of mankind until the Industrial Revolution changed the way of life in Europe some two hundred years ago. Reduced to its basic terms, this revolution in the Middle East amounted to the development of new farming methods that were to prove so successful that for the first time in human history man was able to produce a surplus of food. This simple transforming economic fact had profound social consequences; to start with, it led to a rapid increase in population and at the same time enabled some people to be freed from the hitherto general chore of growing food, making it possible for some to specialise in making the sort of tools which the new farming methods cried out for. These craftsmen in order to provide these tools which the farmers required, needed raw materials, to supply which there came into existence a trading class, which was also drawn from the ranks of those whose services were no longer required for the production of food.

This new society that emerged from this first division of labour comprised farmers, craftsmen and traders. The fresh ideas which animated this new society passed, albeit slowly, from the Middle East to Europe, partly because the increased population looked for somewhere to live, partly because the traders were searching in distant places for supplies of the vital raw materials and partly because some farmers, having exhausted their lands, were ever on the look out for untilled lands to bring into cultivation. The further west these neolithic men emigrated in their varying quests, the simpler were the changes they brought, until when they finally crossed into these islands, they brought with them only the basic knowledge of mixed farming and simple skills in weaving and in making pots. In their flimsy cross-channel boats however, were very precious cargoes indeed, sheep, cattle and the seeds of wheat. These early neolithic men and women, who probably came in quite small groups, were the first settlers in Wales; those that were in Wales before them, the mesolithic hunters and fishers had been nomadic in habit. They hunted and fished for a season before moving on to stalk other quarries and search unknown streams. The neolithic settlers by way of contrast lived in communities, where the general practice seems to have been for the men to look after the animals while the women were held responsible for the growing of the crops. Most of what is now known about the social life of New Stone Age people comes from the excavation of their burial places. Nomads had no cemeteries, individuals being buried where they died, whereas the long barrow, which is the chief clue today to a neolithic settlement, is really a roofed cemetery, in fact the village burial ground.

As the infiltration into Wales of neolithic groups probably continued for more than two thousand years, which is twice as long a period of time as that which covers all English history since the Battle of Hastings, it is hardly surprising that there was considerable variation in the types of graves used and indeed even in the shape of the covering mounds, which tended in the later years of neolithic settlement to be round rather than long. Most neolithic chambered tombs consisted of a number of burial compartments, linked by passages or galleries and roofed over with huge capstones. When such a cemetery was full it was covered over with a large mound of earth. As these early people deemed it wise to bury with their dead a selection of tools and utensils used in life, skilled modern excavation has revealed much valuable information about the neolithic way of life.

At this stage it is necessary to introduce the topic of the Druids about whom more nonsense has been written than about flying saucers! Readers, who are uncertain about them, are advised to read Stuart Piggot's book *The Druids*, which once and for all puts fact and fiction into proper perspective. The historical Druids, who flourished in the early Iron Age, constituted a Celtic priesthood whose activities are recorded from the second century B.C. Nevertheless many a prehistoric ruin has in the public mind become associated with the Druids, none more so than stone circles and bare cromlechs, standing up alone on bleak moors. A cromlech, that is to say upright stones, linked by a heavy capstone, is often all that remains of a neolithic burial place from which the covering mound has been eroded by the combined efforts of time and the vandals, one burial chamber, alone in survival, bearing witness to the former cemetery, that antedated the Druids by several thousand years.

The earliest such communal burial places in Wales are to be found not far from the west coast, suggesting a close connection with the people who at about the same time were settling in Ireland. Dyfed, Gwynedd and Anglesey provide excellent examples of such early burials, details of which will be given later. Suffice it here to mention four outstanding specimens, which, thanks to skilful excavation and in two of the cases to partial restoration, can be seen and appreciated by those who possess the twin advantages of imagination and a motor-car! Of these chosen representatives of the earliest neolithic settlements in Wales one is to be found in Dyfed, at Pentre Ifan, not far from Cardigan, another above the Conwy Valley at Capel Garmon, while, the other two are in Anglesey; one is Bryn Celli Ddu in the south of the island, the other is Barclodiad-y-Gawres, near Rhosneigr in the north-west.

Later neolithic infiltrations into the western part of Britain, dating from about 2000 B.C., were of people from the south of Brittany, who either settled in the Cotswolds or crossed the Severn before making their homes in South Wales. Their graves are categorised as belonging to the Severn-Cotswold type, good Welsh examples of which can be seen at Tinkinswood, which is between Cardiff and Barry, and in the Gower Peninsula at Parc Cwm. At about this same time something very remarkable indeed was taking place further west into Wales in the Presely Hills, where a band of very strong neolithic men dug out of the mountain side the so-called blue stones. These stones, which were to be found nowhere else in the British Isles, were used to form the smaller circle at Stonehenge, though how and why they were transported from the mountains of South Wales to the centre of Salisbury Plain no man yet knows.

As to neolithic artefacts there is considerable archaeological evidence of domestic pottery, while by the end of neolithic times men had learned how to make drinking vessels also by using clay. The most numerous artefacts to survive are finely-made flint arrow-heads and polished stone axes. Certainly by the middle of the New Stone Age a properly-organised trade in stone axes had been developed in North Wales, the necessary raw materials being provided by — doubtless among others — stone axe factories on the Llŷn Peninsula at Mynydd Rhiw (G.R. 234299) and on the eastern end of Penmaenmawr Mountain at Graig Lyd (G.R. 717750).

The Beaker Folk

Somewhere about the beginning of the second millenium B.C. new immigrants came upon the scene, whose forebears had begun a long, restless trek to the west and south of the continent from the forest clearings of eastern Europe, where they had first made their appearance in about 10,000 B.C. The advance parties of these strangers crossed from the mainland of Europe in about 2000 B.C. and landed along the eastern and southern coasts of Britain, gradually thereafter penetrating inland. Of the very many immigrants who eventually infiltrated into Wales, large numbers may well have travelled, albeit by easy stages, via the high lands of Shropshire.

Something of the initial impact made by the arrival of these newcomers on the neolithic inhabitants of North Wales can be imagined from the contrast presented by their different appearance; for these people were light of hair and fair of complexion, and were much taller and much heavier than the small dark residents of North Wales whom they were gradually to dispossess. These new settlers have sometimes been identified with the so-called Beaker Folk, whose name was derived from the distinctive cups that were foremost among their grave goods. In fact these beakers would more accurately be associated with late neolithic men and women, but as there is unlikely to have been any clear-cut division between late neolithic and early Bronze Age times little damage will be done if the term Beaker

Folk is applied both to late neolithic and early Bronze Age men and women.

The association of these beakers with the Bronze Age however cries out for an explanation, especially as most of the new arrivals brought with them no metal goods of any description nor had they in all probability any knowledge of their existence. Nevertheless by coming to these islands when they did, they were very soon made aware of the existence of metal objects because at that time Ireland had achieved a considerable reputation for the excellence of its metal workers, who had learned how to take full advantage of the copper deposits of Kerry and of the alluvial gold to be found in the Wicklow Mountains. Knowledge of the products of these Irish smiths travelled quickly along well-known trade routes, reaching the ears of the fair-haired newcomers to Wales, who were aggressive by nature and thereafter quickly able to recognise the superiority of metal weapons over those made of stone. At this stage in their development they were more interested in the ways of war than in the paths of agricultural peace, quietly trodden by the neolithic people. Thus Wales became an expanding export market for Irish tools and weapons, chief among which were axes and daggers of bronze, and in later Bronze Age times, when life had become rather more civilised, for Irish copper and gold ornaments and decorations.

Of the settling-in process of these people little is known beyond the bare fact that there was an initial clash in which the greater strength of the invaders gave them the mastery. There was however probably more infiltration than confrontation, especially as a beneficent change in climate around 2000 B.C. which resulted in warmer, drier conditions, opened up for settlement higher areas in Wales than had been available for their neolithic predecessors. Illustrations of this are plentifully at hand in central Wales, where in the Brecon Beacons Bronze Age round barrows have been found more than 2000 feet above sea level. Nevertheless there is archaeological evidence too to prove that Bronze Age men took over existing neolithic settlements: high up above the Conwy Valley the long barrow at Capel Garmon, which for so long had been the communal burial ground of a neolithic community, revealed to twentieth century man red fragments of a beaker which have been carbon-dated 1500 B.C. Clearly a neolithic site had been taken over by men of the Bronze Age, just as in much later times it was again to be occupied by Iron Age settlers, who were thus to maintain a continuity of occupation at Capel Garmon.

The Bronze Age was to last in Wales for about fifteen hundred years; this vast expanse of time will have witnessed many invasions and infiltrations of new groups, coming in by a variety of routes. Settlement in Wales in the early years will probably have been sparse, bearing in mind the distance between Wales and the south and east coasts of Britain, where the first landings of these people had been made. However by about 1500 B.C., when Bronze Age culture was at its peak, a fairly clear picture emerges of Bronze Age settlements in Wales, by which time many groups had crossed the Denbighshire moors for some to settle above the Conwy Valley or west of the Rhinogs, while others penetrated into the Llŷn Peninsula or crossed into Anglesey. Other groups had ventured into central areas, settling either in the river valleys of Powys or on the hills and moorlands above, where they were to pursue their pastoralist ways. For, by 1500 B.C. the former warriors had become rearers of cattle and successful farmers, who seem to have been particularly attracted by the hills and valleys of eastern Wales, where today many a skyline is broken by unexcavated round barrows, which also abound in the Teme Valley north of Knighton and around New Radnor, where at the side of the A44 may still be seen a round barrow, fittingly sited in a farmyard, indicating continuity of occupation for two and a half thousand years. Further into Wales, up in the Brecon Beacons National Park, at much greater heights, there is a wealth of archaeological evidence of middle Bronze Age activity, just as there is in many parts of Dyfed, from the high land around Llandeilo and Llandovery *(Llanymddyfri)*, further south to the Presely Hills and to the area north of Carmarthen, just inland from the southern coast.

The contrast between neolithic and Bronze Age man was apparent not only in their physical appearance but also in their burial customs, for, whereas the long barrows of neolithic times were the burial grounds of whole communities, the round barrows of the Bronze Age people, who came after them, covered one or at most two bodies. This change in habit reflected not only the nomadic ways of early Bronze Age settlers but also, and more importantly, the elitist nature of their social structure. For, it appears that only the head man and perhaps his wife had their graves marked by an earthen mound. It is significant that long after Bronze Age man had ceased his nomadic ways, the custom of burying the dead in separate graves continued.

In the early years of the Bronze Age inhumation was still being practised, the body usually being laid on its side in a crouched position, often in a cist of small stones. A mound of earth was then thrown over it, into the sides of which in later years additional burials were sometimes made. By middle Bronze Age times, about 1500 B.C., cremation had taken the place of inhumation; thereafter the ashes were usually stored in cinerary urns or in clay pots. At Bryncir, five miles north of Cricieth in the Llŷn Peninsula, on two different sites at different times cinerary urns and sepulchral clay pots have been dug up, containing not only Bronze Age ashes but also a small bronze knife and a piece of copper.

Of the religious beliefs of the Bronze Age people very little is known for certain beyond the acceptance of the idea of life after death, which is proved by their choice of grave goods. That ritual played some part in their lives can be presumed from the varying practices in vogue at different times in connection with their burials. It is thought that unlike their neolithic predecessors who apparently worshipped the earth, these people believed in a sky god, perhaps the sun and probably held their religious observances in the stone circles, which are the most striking of all Bronze Age monuments and certainly the most puzzling. Professor Thom is the chief exponent of the theory that these stone circles were virtually astronomical clocks, being laid out with such precision that skilled practitioners could from noting accurately the position of the sun, the moon and the stars acquire valuable foreknowledge which was of great service to sailors and farmers. Other Bronze Age survivals that may have figured prominently in their religious rituals were the solitary standing stones that are often to be found in remote places, and cup marks that have been carved on slabs of rock or on chambered tombs or occasionally on standing stones; indeed these strange marks can be found carved on almost any surface regarded by Bronze Age man as sacred.

The first Welshmen

By 1500 B.C. the Bronze Age had become consolidated, its habits and customs and rituals crystallised into a more or less unified culture. The thousand years of Bronze Age culture that followed remained a well-established way of life until Celtic invaders appeared in about 500 B.C. These men were to become the first Welshmen and it was these people who introduced the Iron Age in which we still live.

About halfway through the last millenium before the Christian era mankind was once again on the march in Europe: successive waves of new immigrants, some of whom may well have been refugees, broke against the oft-visited shores of the British Isles. Many of these newcomers, whose homes were in the south-west of Germany or in Switzerland, were the descendants of men who had forged trading links with the people of the east Mediterranean, including the Greeks, traces of whose language were present in the language they spoke. Their culture was associated with La Tène, an area in the Lake Neuchatel district of Switzerland. Their main expansion route to the north was via Belgium and the north of France to the British Isles, though other infiltrations were probably also taking place by sea directly from the Iberian Peninsula to south Wales. At about the same time too other Celts, known as the Gauls, were moving south through Alpine passes to challenge first the authority of the Etruscans in northern Italy and later that of Rome itself.

At least three groups of invaders reached Wales in the early years of this new age. These people were credited in after years with having introduced the Iron Age because they were familiar with the hard metal, and had craftsmen in their midst who knew how to make tools and weapons from it. Nevertheless it would be misleading to say that the early harbingers of this new age depended on this new metal. In fact for a long time in all probability they depended far more on bronze than on iron, sources of which had first to be discovered in these islands, but whether these people concentrated on bronze or on iron, one thing is certainly true, namely that they paid far more attention to making weapons of war than to forging tools of peace. For the Celts came as warriors and for a long time fought their way, often among rival groups of the same tribe.

The Celts came to Wales at a time of flux: to add to the confusion, stirred up by the arrival of a succession of warlike tribes, bent on imposing their will, there was coincidentally another climatic change which brought much colder weather to which considerable adjustment was required. Of the Celts who eventually gained authority in Wales and who spoke a language recognisable as the ancestor of modern Welsh, four particular tribes seem to have gained the ascendancy: the Demetae and the Silures in the south of the country, and the Deceangli and the Ordovices in the north.

Thanks to the skills developed by archaeologists in excavating neolithic and Bronze Age sites and to the interpretative powers of prehistorians, a great deal is now known about the neolithic and Bronze Age ways of life through the patient study of their burial mounds and the grave goods contained therein. Men of the Iron Age unfortunately paid little attention to ritual in disposing of their dead; in consequence little has been gleaned from their burial places. In the Iron Age there were no field monuments corresponding to the barrows, the standing stones and the great stone circles of earlier cultures, though admittedly Iron Age people were very expert at fortifying their settlements, a topic that will be dealt with later. However, despite the lack of field monuments, other than hill forts, much is known about life in the Iron Age because the Iron Age was overlapped by the Roman conquest of Britain. Roman chroniclers in the persons of the general, Julius Caesar and the historian,Tacitus put much on record about the Celts, who dared to oppose their rule in the last century before the Christian era and in the first after it started, by which time the Celtic occupation of Wales was thorough and complete. Of life in Celtic Wales in the centuries before the Romans came to conquer and to chronicle, very little is known, though it is clear that they changed the pattern of agricultural settlement.

The Celtic way of life

The Celts for the first time imposed on the countryside of Wales a clear pattern of settlement, a pattern which was to be dominated and controlled by what are called forts, the types of which varied considerably according to the requirements of differing geographical locations. In previous cultures the land set apart for the cultivation of food was little more than scratched because of the limitations imposed by digging sticks and hand hoes. The meagre crops produced by these primitive methods caused farmers frequently to move on, to cultivate virgin plots of land. The Celts changed all this: to start with, once they had found convenient sources of the precious new metal, iron, they could make stronger agricultural implements. Furthermore by this time they had learned how to make a rudimentary plough, to which the Celts harnessed a pair of oxen. Thus the rectangular Celtic field system was established, whose chief social consequence was the abandoning by farmers of their previous nomadic habits. The farmers thereafter settled near their fields, built themselves huts and gradually coalesced into communities. Their fields were usually bounded by walls made from the stones turned up in the ploughing. This new Celtic pattern of farming in the early centuries of the Iron Age thus gave rise to something approaching a social revolution insofar as a real change in relationship developed between the people and their land, resulting in a quite different way of life. This new social format required proper protection, which was to be afforded by a vast number of forts of differing kinds in differing situations.

Of the very large number of such protected sites to be found in Wales most are quite small, enclosing probably less than one hectare (about two and a half acres), but their very number must prompt an enquiry as to the reason for the need for protection on so wide a scale. Against whom were the settlers protecting themselves? Intense tribal rivalry, in the absence of any central authority (such as before very long the Romans were to try to impose) plus the ability afforded by the possession of iron weapons to mount an attack probably accounted for the proliferation of these forts. In hilly districts much use was made of natural defensive advantages, such as spurs and outcrops of rock which acted as ramparts while occasionally pointed stones were set close together by the defenders to act as an additional deterrent to any invader. Such a device is known as a *chevaux-de-frise*, an excellent example of which is to be seen on the Pen-y-gaer fort in the Conwy Valley.

In coastal areas defences were usually required only on the landward side; as an example of such a promontory fort, Nash Point *(Yr As Fach)* in Glamorgan may be cited (G.R. 915684). While practically nothing of the interior has survived the erosion of the centuries, the entrance is still clear. Any would-be attacker would have had to overcome a succession of four ramparts before gaining access to the track which led to the actual entrance, which presumably would have been well guarded. Two of the commonest type of hill forts have been selected for special comment, one, Ffridd Faldwyn, because it was in use for a very long time, the other, Tre'r Ceiri, because it not only looks very impressive but also because it does so much to increase our knowledge of an Iron Age community.

First to Montgomery, which is worth a visit on several counts. It is a small Georgian town from which noise and bustle have ebbed. The Post Office serves also as a draper's shop and the early closing day is Saturday! Above the well-cared for little town is a castle on a hill which still dominates the landscape as it has done for centuries, but behind and above the castle is another hill, today well-wooded, Ffridd Faldwyn, the site of many a habitation. Its origins were neolithic but in the third century B.C. the Celts arrived to add to the defences of the hill a double palisade. Archaeologists who have found four more Iron age fortifications on the hill, attribute the last of them to the sudden threat posed by the arrival of the Romans in the neighbourhood in about 50 AD. Enough has been excavated to enable an appreciation to be made of three centuries of Iron Age activity there.

Tre'r Ceiri to the layman is the most interesting of all Iron Age forts. Yr Eifl, incorrectly anglicized into The Rivals, is a mountain of three peaks at the eastern end of the Llŷn Peninsula; the most easterly of these three peaks is Tre'r Ceiri, appropriately named, meaning the 'town of the giants'. Here at a height of more than eighteen hundred feet is to be seen an astonishing survival of Celtic building in Wales. The fort is long and narrow, about eight hundred feet in length and about three hundred feet wide; its walls are surprisingly well-preserved, about six feet thick in some places and here and there between ten and fifteen feet high. Remarkable however as are these walls and the three postern gates in them, pride of place must be given to the hundred and fifty huts in the space enclosed by the walls; their varying shapes from circular to square help to confirm the theory that their building was spread over several centuries. Dating the fort is difficult but it seems certain that it remained inhabited throughout the Roman occupation of Britain.

The Druids

The Romans, whose initial reconnaisance on the shores of southern Britain in 55 B.C. was followed by an army of occupation in 43 A.D., entered Wales in about 50 A.D. Their conquest was opposed by the Celts, who were sufficiently well-organised to constitute a threat to Roman plans. The Silures in the south and the Ordovices in the north by their spirited resistance reminded the Romans of the trouble they had previously experienced at the hands of the Celts in their earlier conquest of Gaul. The further the Celts were from the centre of Roman government, the greater was their determination to resist. Hence it was that the Roman general, Suetonius Paulinus set himself the task of subduing Anglesey, the very centre of Celtic resistance and the headquarters of Druidism.

The Druids were a priestly caste of Celts whose leadership, though basically spiritual, had spread over into the realm of political power. According to Tacitus potential Celtic leaders were sent from distant Celtic domains in Europe to Anglesey, where they were taught and trained and indoctrinated in Druid lore which had become the official religion of all Celts everywhere. These Druid leaders seemingly constituted a hierarchy of enormous importance; they taught religion and astronomy, history and philosophy and were held in the greatest veneration by the rest of the Celts over whom they exercised a very tight discipline. Unfortunately for posterity however all their teaching was oral, which left the way clear for romantics down the centuries to indulge their imaginations. In fact practically nothing is known of what the Druids taught. All that is known for certain is that the Celts in Wales, thanks to their Druid advisers in Anglesey, were utterly opposed to the overlordship of Rome and that the Romans decided in consequence to destroy Druidism root and branch.

In 61 A.D. Suetonius Paulinus, with more than a little trepidation, crossed into Anglesey and advanced upon the sacred groves of the Druids in the middle of the island where he burned all the trees and killed all the priests. He was recalled from this act of butchery by news of *Boudicca's* rising in eastern Britain but, although he had not succeeded in breaking the power of the Celts, he had destroyed their power base, the priesthood of the Druids.

Barclodiad y Gawres: near Rhosneigr, in Anglesey. A torch is necessary if the visitor is to see those stones which are decorated with chevrons etc. indicating a cultural affinity with Ireland.

Bryn-celli-ddu: near Llanddaniel-fab in Anglesey. A cultural centre of outstanding importance both in the neolithic and the Bronze Age.

B. THE ARCHAEOLOGICAL RECORD

The most ancient surviving sites in Wales of human habitations, however temporary, are to be found in Clwyd. Earliest of all, carbon-dated to about 180,000 B.C. is near Y Bontnewydd, in a cave, about four miles north-west of Denbigh and three miles south-west of St. Asaph, the G.R. being 015710. This cave, which is not normally open to the public, is cut into the limestone cliff which dominates the north side of the river Elwy. First excavated in 1872, it has in recent years been thoroughly surveyed by the National Museum of Wales. Many implements, mostly made of quartzite, have been found there together with some human bones.

A few miles further east lies the village of Tremeirchion, a mile south of which are to be found two important caves, very near to each other. One is called Ffynnon Beuno, the other Cae Gwyn (G.R. 085724). Both sites, when excavated about a hundred years ago, yielded up a few human and a great many animal bones; the caves are thought to have been the homes of hyenas, many of whose bones have survived along with the remains of the animals they killed, like woolly rhinoceros and mammoth. In addition flint implements were also found which enabled archaeologists to give a date to the site somewhere between 50,000 and 30,000 B.C. Cae Gwyn is now quite inaccessible but with care Ffynnon Beuno may be explored.

Palaeolithic remains in the Gower Peninsula are of much more recent habitations than those of the limestone caves of the north. 16,500 B.C. is the approximate date given to the earliest human being found in the Gower Peninsula, that of the skeleton of the

Capel Garmon: North of Betws-y-coed and near the village of the same name. Probably in use for an ever greater period of time than Bryn-celli-ddu, as an Iron Age fire-dog was discovered there (now on exhibition in the National Museum in Cardiff).

Dyffryn Ardudwy: Between Harlech and Barmouth, behind the school at Dyffryn. The whole area is rich in prehistoric sites.

young Cro-Magnon man, formerly known as the Red Lady of Paviland; the Grid Reference for the Goat's Hole, where it was found, is 437858. Paviland lies east of Worms Head in the south of the peninsula along the coast between Rhossili and Port Einon. Access to this cave is from the shore but only at low tide. It appears to have been used by man and beast for a great many years, the earliest animal occupation probably antedating the arrival of humans there by about ten thousand years, while archaeological evidence also suggests much later occupation in mesolithic, neolithic and even in Roman times.

Also in the Gower Peninsula a visit is recommended to Cat Hole (G.R. 538900), an inland rock shelter above a wooded valley, north-west of Oxwich in the parish of Ilston. The earliest occupation is thought to have been about 10,000 B.C. It appears from the evidence afforded by numerous flints found there that a substantial flint industry flourished there in late palaeolithic times. There have been a number of excavations of the site from which it has been deduced that mesolithic men also sheltered there in later years, while later again men of the Bronze Age chose to bury their dead in this rock shelter.

As the ice melted (somewhere around 9,000 B.C.), the weather gradually became warmer, and the vegetation grew lush and in consequence the caves and rock shelters became dark and wet and no longer habitable. Men and women had to leave their homes and somehow learn how to adjust to the changed environment. These so-called Mesolithic or Middle Stone Age people were hunters who came to depend for their survival on killing the new animals that had been attracted by the deciduous woodland that had spread as the ice retreated. Of these animals the most important were the red deer. Man had by this time acquired sufficient technique to make small sharp barbs from their flakes of flint. Armed with these microliths, which they attached to sticks, they hunted down the deer that roamed the woodland. Small collections of these microliths have been found both in Clwyd and in Glamorgan. In Clwyd those found at Rhuddlan have been carbondated to about 6,500 B.C. while those discovered near Prestatyn are thought to have been fashioned about fifteen hundred years later.

Tinkinswood and St Lythans: Near neighbours, west of Cardiff, in Glamorgan. In use in late neolithic and Bronze Age times.

High up under the Mynydd Hiraethog in Clwyd the deliberate flooding of the Brenig Valley was completed in 1976 (G.R. 985576). Fortunately, the architects of the scheme took archaeologists into their confidence and the result was that very valuable prehistoric sites were not only identified and excavated but also protected for posterity. A series of trails has been devised by the Welsh Water Authority with accompanying maps and markers. From the central car park one of these trails leads to a mesolithic summer camp, suitably marked. A sunny day spent at the Llyn Brenig Reservoir would reveal to the discerning visitor many prehistoric sites of widely differing periods and cultures.

In a later chapter the short sea crossing from Tenby in Dyfed to Caldey Island will be strongly recommended in order to study some early Christian memorial stones of outstanding interest. This same holy island (it is now the home of a monastic community, members of which are well-disposed towards historically-minded visitors) also possesses a number of mesolithic sites, amongst which are Nanna's Cave (G.R. 145960) and Porter's Cave (G.R. 143971).

Very many neolithic sites have been identified in Wales, some of which now only exist in vestigial traces. In this section a selection has been made, in compiling which attention has been given both to their intrinsic interest and to their geographical spread. Moving from north to south the first sites to be mentioned are those in Anglesey, where there are so many that it is invidious to make a choice.

Halfway up the east coast of the island, behind Benllech lies the village of Tyn-y-gongl, above which on rising ground is Pant-y-saer (G.R. 509824). It has been excavated twice; there remains today a large sloping capstone, supported by low stones, which cover a burial pit, cut into the rock. Here more than forty skeletons were found and some neolithic pottery.

On the opposite coast, a mile and a half south-east of Holyhead, between the A5 and B4545, is the long barrow, Trefignath (G.R. 258805). A car may be left about a hundred yards from the site which until recently was regarded as a good example of a passage grave, subdivided into several chambers,

Penrhos Feilw: On Holy Island, S.W. of Holyhead. This pair of tall thin stones presents a mystery; tradition has it that at one time they were in the middle of a stone circle. There is too a local legend that a stone cist, full of bones and artefacts, was dug up between the stones, but until archaeologists dig the site, the mystery will remain.

Pentre Ifan: Inland from Nevern, in Dyfed. One of the best known and most photographed prehistoric burial places in South Wales.

the whole being similar to segmented graves found in parts of Ireland and in the south of Scotland. This view was supported by the visual remains which principally consist of two seven feet high portal stones and a passage some forty-five feet long leading from it. There is little sign of a covering mound which was noted by observers a hundred years ago. Another excavation, between 1977 and 1979, suggests however that the grave is not all of one piece. While it is still believed that the tall portal stones and at least part of the passage belong to an originally mound-covered neolithic long barrow, other remains point to simple burials of other periods.

Of other neolithic sites in that neighbourhood one is less than a mile north of Llanfaelog, off A4080, about two miles inland from Rhosneigr. Tŷ Newydd (G.R. 344738) consists mainly of a large capstone which rests on three uprights. When excavated in 1935, under a fallen stone on the floor were found amongst other things sufficient pieces of post-neolithic pottery to indicate that the neolithic grave was either still in use in the Bronze Age or had been brought back into use by Bronze Age men.

Not far south of Rhosneigr and two miles north-west of Aberffraw is one of the most important and visually striking neolithic sites in the whole of Britain, Barclodiad y Gawres, (G.R. 328708) which is not to be confused with another burial site with an identical name in Gwynedd on the Roman road between Caerhun and Segontium (G.R. 716716). The Anglesey Barclodiad has had to be locked up and a word of caution is necessary concerning the whereabouts of the key which has known a number of homes, the most recent being the custodian's office at Beaumaris Castle in the south-east of the island, where a money deposit has to be left.

Barclodiad y Gawres is wonderfully situated on a headland overlooking Trecastell Bay (Cable Bay) where a car may be left on the foreshore below, before following the signpost which points to the headland a quarter of a mile away. The burial chamber, which was thoroughly excavated in 1953, has been skilfully restored and in the process a concrete dome has been built over it to protect its precious contents from the weather and the wickedness of man. It is essential to take a torch. The grave itself is of the normal neolithic passage type, giving access to a central area on one side of which is a single small chamber and on the other a double one. Unfortunately many stones had been stolen and a great deal of damage done in the years before the excavation took place. What makes the place so exciting today is the survival there of five upright stones with chevrons, spirals and zigzags carved on their surfaces. The stone carvers will have had a cultural affinity with those who settled in Spain and Ireland. The stones themselves are thought to have been glacial erratics, deposited on the headland.

The last neolithic site on Anglesey earmarked for special comment is probably the best known and most famous, Bryn-celli-ddu (G.R. 508702). It is perhaps best to approach it via the A5, turning left at Llanfair PG on to the A4080. A mile along this road turn right on to a minor road, marked Llanddaniel-fab. Before this village is reached a marker will be seen on the righthand side indicating a field track which is barred to cars, leading to Bryn-celli-ddu. At the end of the lane is a farm, where the Department of the Environment pamphlet may be bought, the key to the chamber obtained and a small admission charge paid. The pamphlet is essential if the mysteries of a complicated site are to be at all understood.

Once inside the fenced-in enclosure a restored circular mound is visible. Access through the locked iron door is to a passage grave, in the central chamber of which stands a smooth-faced stone pillar. On the outside of the mound at the back may be seen in a shallow pit a stone (a replica of the original which is housed in the National Museum of Wales in Cardiff). This stone has carved on it spirals and other decorative patterns, reminiscent of Barclodiad y Gawres. The pit which is likely to have witnessed important rituals, originally marked the very middle of the monument.

The visitor who wants to acquire some sense of the size and significance of this outstanding prehistoric monument, should climb on to the top of the mound and realise that the original mound will have covered the whole of the area now enclosed by the wire fence. Bryn-celli-ddu may well have been, as well as a cemetery, an important meeting place. Neolithic men first came here to bury their dead but equally certainly Bronze Age people continued for very many years to use the same site, so that it should be regarded today as much a monument of the Bronze Age as of the New Stone Age.

Between Anglesey and the south, which were the two great centres of early prehistoric settlement in Wales, three neolithic sites claim special attention of which the most northerly is Capel Garmon (G.R. 818542). This burial place ocupies a remote site, high up on the eastern side of the Conwy Valley, well above the road which runs from Betws-y-coed to Llanrwst. Half a mile of country road, south-west of the village of Capel Garmon leads to a widened stretch where a car may be left. A finger post points to a farm where the necessary pamphlet may be obtained, and to the site which enjoys a spectacular view of the distant hills the other side of the valley.

This neolithic long barrow is shaped like a wedge, a horned forecourt at the east end luring unwanted strangers in former times to a false entrance, the true approach being from the south via a passage at the end of which were two burial chambers, one to the west, the other to the east. The excavation of 1924 revealed, along with neolithic remains, sufficient pottery to prove that Bronze Age people continued to use the site long after neolithic men and women had passed from the scene.

The next site to be explored is near the A496, the coast road which goes from Harlech to Barmouth. Just south of the village of Dyffryn Ardudwy the remains of the long barrow, bearing the same name, will be found, behind the village school (G.R. 589229). This is indeed a place of stones, suggesting that the burial place was here roofed with stones rather than by the usual grassy mounds of earth. There are the remains of two burial places, the smaller, earlier one is the more westerly, its outline clearly marked out in the stones on the ground. The other, slightly later, was very much bigger. It is probable that one roof of stones will have covered both graves, in which archaeologists have found early neolithic pottery.

In western Powys, in central Wales, is an unusual long barrow, unusual because it is perched up on the edge of a ridge, Tŷ Illtud (reference to this name will be made in the third chapter of this book, when the Celtic Church is under consideration). The actual site (G.R. 098263) is in a field, belonging to Manest Farm, which is situated a mile up a minor road which leaves the A40 four miles south-east of Brecon at the village of Scethrog. Permission must be sought at the farm to visit the site, which is visible from the lane, a brisk walk away up the hill. Special interest is centred on the partly-roofed forecourt on the wallstones on which have been carved, probably in medieval times, patterns which in the course of time have greatly exercised the minds and imaginations of many visitors.

Moving south into Dyfed pride of place must go to Pentre Ifan (G.R. 099370) seven miles south-west of Cardigan; it stands in a field, near a lane, which is roughly equidistant between the A487 and the B4329. The surviving entrance to this chambered tomb consists of three pillars, eight feet high, surmounted by an immense capstone, sixteen feet long, in front of which is a forecourt, semi-circular in shape. The covering mound will have been about one hundred and thirty feet long. The unusual orientation was north-south, as it also was at Ty Illtud. Traces of ritual pits are visible, the purpose of which is frequently guessed at but at this distance of time hardly likely to be known.

Neolithic remains abound in the coastal area between Strumble Head and St David's, suggesting a safe anchorage and considerable settlement. Let one such site speak for them all, Carreg Samson (G.R. 846334) in the parish of Mathry, lying seven miles to the south-west of Fishguard, near Abercastle, and occupying a splendid position overlooking the bay. Today all that remains of a long barrow, which originally was probably covered by stones rather than by grass, are seven upright stones, roofed by a capstone. Inland along this coast another ten similar neolithic sites may be found.

Three more neolithic sites to be visited are further east, in Glamorgan, the first of which is in the Gower Peninsula, an area which is rich in archaeological remains. Parc Cwm (G.R. 537898) is a long barrow of the Severn-Cotswold type, situated inland in the peninsula between B4271 and A4118. First recognised as a neolithic burial place in 1869, in 1960 it was thoroughly and scientifically excavated. On a north-south alignment, it has a forecourt shaped like a bell which gives access to a central gallery off which are four side-chambers. Over the years the bones of about twenty-four people have been recovered, suggesting that Parc Cwm was a communal burial place, a cemetery with a roof on! It is a spectacular site.

The other two sites are near each other, a few miles to the west of Cardiff and south of the road which runs westwards from Cardiff to Cowbridge — Tinkinswood and St Lythan's *(Llwyneliddon)*. Tinkinswood (G.R. 092732) was excavated in 1914 and afterwards carefully restored. The burial chamber is covered by an immense capstone, believed to be the largest in Britain, measuring twenty-two feet by fifteen; the bones of about fifty people were found, along with flints, pottery and a quantity of animal bones — the presence of the latter arguing the likelihood of funeral feasting. In the mound was discovered another of those mysterious pits, often come across in long barrows, mysterious because no one knows anything about them. Tinkinswood was probably a late neolithic burial place which was subsequently re-used by men of the early Bronze Age some of whose pottery has been unearthed there.

A mile to the south-east is the long barrow of St Lythan's (G.R. 101723) a visit to which may be justified by its proximity to Tinkinswood. The elements have here reduced the original long mound of stones to three uprights supporting a capstone, which stands out gauntly in the middle of a field. The Department of the Environment has produced an excellent combined brochure which deals with both these sites.

There are no surviving Bronze Age settlements in Wales: the four types of visual evidence all have to do with ritual and death, three of them posing as yet unsolved mysteries concerning the reasons why Bronze Age people periodically foregathered in stone circles, why they set up in lonely places solitary tall stones and why they carved on some of their monuments curious shapes to which archaeologists have given the name cupmarks. Their places of burial were much smaller and less complicated than were those of the neolithic people they supplanted; most of such places in Wales are simple mounds or piles of stones under which were found human bones which in the early years of the Bronze

Ysbyty Cynfyn: North of Devil's Bridge in N. Dyfed. The present 19th c. church is the successor to a much earlier church, built into the western side of a Bronze Age circular enclosure. Nowhere is there to be found a better example of the continuity of religious association.

Four Stones: In Powys, north of Old Radnor, south of the hamlet of Kinnerton. This puzzling group of glacial erratics has been the subject of much local folk-lore.

Age were buried, cremation taking over in about 1500 B.C. Sometimes the bones, cremated or otherwise, accompanied by simple grave goods, such as flint knives or beads or small drinking vessels, were placed in stone cists, the walls of which consisted of large slabs. The covering mounds of these round barrows were of grass-topped soil or of stone. Their distribution was widespread, both on hill-tops and in fertile valleys, though there seems to have been something of a concentration in one part of north-west Wales. Bronze Age remains of various sorts, have been unearthed at Penrhyndeudraeth, on the slopes of Cnicht, around Bryncir and at Beddgelert and at Dolwyddelan, prompting the theory that the area around the Glaslyn Estuary was a major Bronze Age settlement. Today's visitor has to bear in mind that the river Glaslyn was a wide tidal river which flowed as far east as the western slopes of Cnicht until the early years of the nineteenth century when W. A. Madocks built an embankment across the mouth of the estuary, which was to link Meirionnydd to the Caernarfonshire side and make possible the development of a harbour at Porthmadog.

In addition to round barrows there are a number of other Bronze Age burial sites which consist of a mound or several mounds, surrounded by a ditch and bank; to such the name of Wessex bell-barrow is given. The people responsible for creating these burial mounds are thought to have had strong cultural ties with a prosperous Bronze Age culture centred in Wessex. Remains of some of these bell-barrows are to be found in Glamorgan, especially in the district around Llanilltud Fawr (Llantwit Major) in the south, though there is an outstanding example in the north of the county, Crug-yr-Afan (G.R. 920954). Oddly enough there is a bell-barrow in North Wales too, in the hilly country behind Llanfairfechan, Cors y Carneddau (G.R. 723746).

The hilly uplands of Clwyd and Powys are still dotted with unexcavated round barrows but a great many have been obliterated in the course of the centuries by the weather and the plough. In Gwynedd the energetic hill walker who climbs up westward out of the Conwy Valley to walk along the ridge from Foel Grach towards the sea will be rewarded with the sight of two

Old Radnor: One mile south of Four Stones, in Powys. Today's parish church, which stands on the site of a very early church, rears itself up on the top of a mound, itself surrounded by a very considerable Bronze Age earthwork.

round barrows, one near the top of Drum, Carnedd Penyborth-goch (G.R. 708696), the other a mile or so further on, Carnedd Y Ddelw (G.R. 708705).

Another rewarding but less tiring excursion may be undertaken in the Mynydd Hiraethog in Clwyd, where a few years ago the northern part of the Brenig Valley was flooded by the Welsh Water Authority. During the building of the reservoir archaeologists were called in who identified and excavated many Bronze Age sites, some of which have been restored and resited north-east of Llyn Brenig, where they form part of a trail, which the authorities have carefully laid out, starting at the car park. There are other Bronze Age sites in the park which are described and routed in a brochure obtainable at the information centre behind the car park.

One more round barrow, quite differently sited, is worth a mention — and a visit, though it involves a steep walk along a mountain path. The visitor to the excellent Mountain Centre at Libanus will see on the eastern horizon the twin peaks of the Brecon Beacons. The barrow, Corn Du, where a cist has been excavated is at a height of 2863 feet, on the side of the western summit (G.R. 007213).

Stone circles are always associated with the Bronze Age, even though nothing is known for certain what went on within their undoubtedly sacred confines. Wales has nothing to offer to compare with the magnificence of Castlerigg near Keswick or of Long Meg near Penrith, but there are a number of small stone circles still surviving, mostly concentrated in the hilly uplands of Powys. Jaquetta Hawkes says this of them, "...looking at them in the loneliness and grandeur of the mountain country in which they so often stand we have to imagine them a centre of movement, colour, vitality and emotion."

Three such circles in the mountain country west and south-west of Brecon may be visited in one day, of which the most southerly and the best is Cerrig Duon, (G.R. 852206), which stands out at a height of 1270 feet, not far from the source of the river Tawe. The circle consists of twenty-two stones (there are about eight gaps); none of the stones is higher than about eighteen inches, the whole perimeter measuring about one

Harold's Stones: Tryleg is a village, 7 miles south of Monmouth, on the west side of the Wye Valley. Why these stones were erected no-one knows; they are accepted as belonging to the Bronze Age and may in earlier times have formed part of a larger alignment. A sun-dial in the village church, dated 1689, has on it a carving of these stones.

Dinllugwy: Inland from Moelfre, on the east coast of Anglesey. This enclosed hut group of the 4th c. A.D. was probably quite unknown to the Roman garrison at Segontium, a few miles away to the south.

hundred and ninety feet. About thirty feet north of the circle is a large standing stone about six feet high, while north-east of the circle are two nearly parallel rows of stones. This alignment clearly stood in some relationship to the circle.

Six miles north of Cerrig Duon and a quarter of a mile to the east of the Roman camp at Y Pigwn is Mynydd Bach Trecastell (G.R. 833310). It is usually permissible to visit the site, although it is actually inside the boundary of the army training centre. Here two circles will be found, the smaller one to the south being twenty-four feet in diameter, the larger seventy-six. There is, as at Cerrig Duon, an alignment of stones, leading away from the southern circle in a south-westerly direction.

The third site lies three miles further south and a mile and a half south of the Usk Reservoir, Nant Tarw (G.R. 819258), which has to be approached on foot over rather rough moorland. Again there are two enclosures, of which one is circular with seven uprights still in position, while the other, elliptical in shape, has twelve surviving stones of which the tallest is three and a half feet high.

North-west Anglesey provides a number of standing stones which are typical enough to speak for the rest that can be seen in many different parts of Wales. At Pen yr Orsedd (G.R. 333903 and 333906) are two specimens, six to seven feet high, while a mile and three quarters north north-east of Bodedern is another at Tregwehelydd. The stone here which is eight and a half feet high, was found in three pieces but is now bolted together. On the nearby Holy Island will be found two more sites, one Ty Mawr (G.R. 254810), one mile south south-east of Holyhead has a nine foot stone, while at Penrhosfeilw (G.R. 227809), one and three-quarters of a mile south-west of Holyhead there are two stones, eleven feet apart, each about ten feet high.

Near Devil's Bridge in the most northerly part of Dyfed is the little 19thc. church of Ysbyty Cynfin, which seems to have been built in the middle of a Bronze Age site. Today's churchyard wall contains five stones, which were a part of the original Bronze Age alignment; two of them have been moved to act as gate-posts, while the other three, one of which is about ten feet high, have probably remained undisturbed since they were first

*Pen-y-gaer: Above the village of Llanbedr-y-cennin in the Conwy Valley, S.W. of the Roman fort Caerhun. This Iron Age hillfort was protected by lines of pointed stones (*cheveux de frise*) on the south and west sides. Remains of 20 huts have been found in the fort.*

Tre'r Ceiri: In the Llŷn Peninsula, west of Llanaelhaearn. Tre'r Ceiri, 'The Town of the Giants' is on the S.W. summit of Yr Eifl.

erected three and a half thousand years ago.

Far away in Powys, near the old boundary between Radnorshire and Herefordshire a few hundred yards north of the A44 at G.R. 245608, are the Four Stones. These are four glacial boulders, set up with their flat surfaces facing the middle. No one knows why they were put up nor what happened there, but half a mile away to the north-east is another similar group of glacial erratics (G.R. 262609)

While in the neighbourhood a further visit is recommended, namely to Old Radnor, which lies one mile to the south of the Four Stones. Old Radnor today consists only of a church, an inn and a few houses, but a visit is well worth while to view one of the biggest and certainly the best parish church in Radnorshire, to ponder on the possible prehistoric origin of what today is the font of the church and above all to marvel at the fact that the church stands on top of Bronze Age earthworks.

Of the mysteries which surround Bronze Age practices none is harder to comprehend than the reason for the so-called cupmarks which were carved on a variety of stone surfaces, though it seems possible that they played some part in burial ritual. Three sites are suggested for visits, one in the Lleyn Peninsula, another near the Pembrokeshire coast and the third in Gwent in the village of Tryleg below Monmouth.

Near Clynnog Fawr, the St David's of North Wales, is a long barrow; on the upper surface of its capstone are no fewer than one hundred and ten cupmarks. Bach-wen (G.R. 407495) is far from easy to find. It is sited on private land with no fingerpost to offer guidance. The lane to the west of the church runs to the coast; two-thirds of the way along it is a 'cross-lanes'. Take the lane to the left which finishes at a gate, beyond which the cromlech may be seen. The search is worth the effort because Bach-wen presents an interesting situation. The mound, be it of soil or stone, that originally covered this neolithic burial place, must have disappeared by Bronze Age times for Bronze Age men to be able to carve their cupmarks on top of the capstone. A similar situation may be observed at Trelyffant (G.R. 082425) in Dyfed. West of the B4582 which runs south-west from Cardigan to Nevern, lie the remains of a long barrow, whose capstone reveals twenty-two cupmarks.

Finally, to the west side of the Wye Valley in Gwent, where Tryleg is situated. Tryleg, at one time the county town of Monmouthshire and in more recent times famed as the birthplace of Bertrand Russell, takes its name from the three stones which have been anachronistically linked with the Saxon Harold, who made war in these parts. Harold's Stones (G.R. 499051) are three in number; they belong to the Bronze Age and lean in different directions, with the middle one bearing two cupmarks on its southern side.

Enough was said in the last chapter about Ffridd Faldwyn and Tre'r Ceiri, the two outstanding Iron Age settlements in Wales, to limit reference here to only their geographical positions. Ffridd Faldwyn (G.R. 216969) is a half a mile west of Montgomery, while Tre'r Ceiri (G.R. 374447) looms up above the A449, which links Caernarfon to Pwllheli, just after the road leaves the north coast, south-west of Clynnog Fawr.

For holiday makers in Anglesey a visit to Llugwy is a very rewarding experience. Cars may be left at Llanallgo, north of Benllech, from where a walk of little more than half a mile in a northerly direction will reveal first a neolithic long barrow, then the interesting ruins of a twelfth century church (with a crypt under the chancel), and finally after a pleasant approach through a wood, a well-hidden Celtic village. Din Llugwy (G.R. 496862) is not the usual type of Iron Age fortification but rather a native village which seems to have been fortified at a later stage in its existence, probably in the fourth century A.D. The half-acre site was enclosed by walls, four to five feet thick, which formed a pentagon. There are the remains of two circular houses and a number of rectangular enclosures, thought to have been used for the smelting of iron.

Another Iron Age fort lies about three miles inland from Port Dinorwig on the North Wales coast, north-east of Caernarfon. The actual site of Dinas Dinorwig (G.R. 550653) is in the uplands a mile south of Llanddeiniolen (on B4366). This Iron Age settlement is likely to have been in use for several centuries, the first settlers having probably dug themselves in before the Romans reached Wales. The subsequent enlarging and strengthening of the fort may well have been occasioned by the building of the Roman station at Segontium, five miles to the south-west, which Dinas Dinorwig overlooked. Although the place is now very much overgrown, there is enough left to suggest that this was a substantial hill fort.

The next hill fort, Craig Rhiweirth (G.R. 057270) beckons only to the adventurous. It is situated on a hill top, overlooking the Tanat Valley in mid-Wales, about a mile north of Llangynog which lies on the B4391, a useful place for leaving a car. On the way up to the top disused lead mines will be seen, which in the eighteenth century produced much high quality ore. The summit where Iron Age Celts chose to settle, is more than adequately protected by nature on all but the north side. Within the defences, both man-made and natural, are to be seen the remains of a large number of stone huts, mostly facing south, in al probability amounting to about a hundred and fifty, but the site has not yet been thoroughly excavated.

Just south of Aberystwyth is a hill on whose upper slopes the first settlers in these parts made their homes. Pendinas (G.R. 584805) has two peaks, which these Celts fortified separately in about 300 B.C., adding in later years a wall which was to enclose them both. The site was apparently occupied for about two hundred years. Today these Iron Age remains share the somewhat incongruous company of a column, consisting of an upended cannon, put there to commemorate victory at Waterloo.

The last site to be dealt with in this section overlooks the Towy Valley, in Carmarthenshire. Carn Goch (G.R. 691243), situated about five miles north east of Llandeilo and about three miles south of Llangadog, is one of the largest hill forts in South Wales. It is over two thousand feet long and about five hundred feet wide; part of the defensive wall stands in places over twenty feet high. Despite its ruinous state this fort still impresses, especially as four gateways are still visible, all lined with upright slabs of stone.

ROMAN INTERLUDE

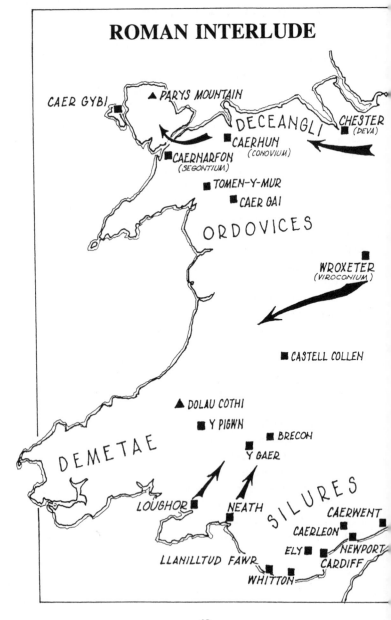

CAER GYBI

▲ PARYS MOUNTAIN

DECEANGLI

CHESTER
(DEVA)

CAERHUN
(CONOVIUM)

CAERNARFON
(SEGONTIUM)

TOMEN-Y-MUR

CAER GAI

ORDOVICES

WROXETER
(VIROCONIUM)

CASTELL COLLEN

▲ DOLAU COTHI

Y PIGWN

BRECON

Y GAER

DEMETAE

SILURES

LOUGHOR

NEATH

CAERWENT

CAERLEON

ELY

NEWPORT

CARDIFF

LLANILLTUD FAWR

WHITTON

ROMAN INTERLUDE

A. FROM 61 TO 383 A.D.

Roman penetration and organisation

The raid into Anglesey, made by Suetonius Paulinus in 61 A.D., to which reference was made in the last chapter, has to be seen as an isolated punitive raid, forced upon the Romans by their very real fear of the influence exercised by the Druid priesthood over the Celts, who were putting up such stout resistance to Roman arms in other parts of southern Britain. The systematic conquest and occupation of Wales could not be attempted until the rest of southern Britain had first been made to toe the line. Hence, although the Roman invaders had landed in Kent in 43 A.D., it was not until 74 that the systematic conquest of Wales could be contemplated. In that year Sextus Julius Frontinus succeeded to the governorship of Britain and wasted little time before mounting an attack against the Silures, whose territory roughly corresponded to Gwent and Glamorgan. Two miles north-east of modern Newport Frontinus made a base and established a military fortress, Isca Silurum (Caerleon), where he quartered the second Augustan legion, five thousand six hundred strong. From Isca he attacked the Silures, who proved to be doughty fighters as the Roman historian Tacitus confirmed. "He (Frontinus)", Tacitus wrote, "defeated the Silures, a strong and aggressive tribe, overcoming a brave enemy and a difficult terrain." In the course of this campaign Frontinus seems to have established bases on tidal estuaries at Neath and

Loughor *(Casllwchwr)*, from which vantage points he was able to provision and reinforce the soldiers in the field. The lands further west than those occupied by the Silures were controlled by the Demetae, whose tribal capital was Carmarthen. The absence of any considerable ruins of Roman fortifications in modern Pembrokeshire and Carmarthenshire suggests that the Demetae presented a lesser military threat to the invaders. The plans and tactics so successfully used by Frontinus in the conquest of Silurian South Wales, however, became models for subsequent imitation when the reduction of the more northerly Ordovices was under consideration.

Four years later Gnaeus Julius Agricola took over from Frontinus and immediately set about the subjugation of the Ordovices, the Deceangli, who inhabited what we know as Clwyd, having already been subdued, one assumes, fairly easily, insofar as there are no traces of Roman forts thereabouts. Based upon Chester, which was the headquarters of the Twentieth legion, Agricola sent out in 74 parties of soldiers, each consisting of from five hundred to a thousand men, who methodically marched westwards, pausing to build the necessary roads and choosing suitable sites for fortifying. One of these forts was established the following year in 75 four and a half miles up the Conwy Valley at Caerhun, which was in later days to be linked with other strong points further south like Tomen y Mur. Caerhun's main importance however was as a staging post on the road to a bigger fort to be built further west, which Agricola selected and had built in the year 78 on high ground above Caernarfon. This remote fort was Segontium, from where the campaign to conquer Anglesey was in the same year launched and speedily brought to a successful conclusion.

Important sites

It is of course one thing for an invading force to conquer a territory and quite another to administer it adequately. The Romans however were nothing if not thorough and painstaking, and they had had a great deal of experience with occupation policy elsewhere. The Romans throughout their long occupation of Wales supervised and controlled the conquered lands from two legionary fortresses, from Chester in the north, which kept under its watchful glance the Deceangli and the Ordovices, and from Caerleon *(Caerllion)* in the south, which maintained Roman law and order among the Demetae and the Silures. The former Silurian and Ordovician lands were administered by Roman officials, who saw to it that forts and fortlets were built at convenient intervals along the excellent roads that Roman engineers had made. Roman Britain as a whole was divided into two zones, the civil and the military, the former enjoying the amenities of the Roman way of life, the latter the attention of the Roman army. The whole of Wales lay in the military zone, save for the south-east corner, where a substantial civilian settlement was established to the east of Caerleon, halfway between modern Newport *(Casnewydd)* and Chepstow. This was Venta Silurum, Caer-went. Originally peopled in all probability by time-expired legionaries from Caerleon, Caer-went became the tribal capital of the Silures and grew to be a splendid civilised place with baths and shops and public buildings, probably second only in importance to Bath in the south-west of Britain. Caer-went was an oasis in a desert of military control, although there is archaeological evidence of the existence of three Roman villas near the south coast, one at Llanilltud Fawr (Llantwit Major), thought to have been built in the middle of the second century A.D., the other two west of Cardiff, one a substantial farm and the other believed to have been concerned with the smelting of iron, also dating from the second century.

With these exceptions civilian life in Roman Wales was limited to the settlements that grew up around the main forts and to the communities engaged in mining, of which three examples will be given. Gold was mined in the area around Pumsaint between Lampeter and Llandeilo (the Dolau Cothi mines); lead was worked in Roman times a few miles north-west of Wrexham in the north, while copper in considerable quantities was taken from Parys Mountain inland from Amlwch in the north-east corner of Anglesey. It is possible that the mineral wealth of Wales was administered by civilians, acting under military jurisdiction, but generally speaking Wales was directly and sternly ruled by the Roman army, units of which, operating from their two great bases, will have patrolled the territory ceaselessly on their well-made roads.

In the next chapter details will be given of surviving visual evidence of the Roman occupation. Here, in the section that follows a few sites will be briefly described either because they were of outstanding importance such as Caerleon and Caer-went or because they were remote like Tomen y Mur or because their remains are now vestigial as at Segontium.

Caerleon, (G.R. 340907) possibly a contraction of Castra Legionum, the Camp of the Legions, was certainly the most important Roman site in Wales, occupying more than fifty acres. Today it is mostly built upon — for instance the local parish church stands in the very middle of the Roman fort on the exact spot which was once adorned by the headquarters of the second Augusta legion. Enough however remains of this spectacular fort, built on the banks of the river Usk, to give a strong impression to today's visitor of the might of Rome in the first century A.D. Giraldus Cambrensis visited Caerleon at the end of the twelfth century and commented thus: "...immense palaces...a lofty tower...remarkable hot baths, the remains of temples and an amphitheatre...wherever you look, you can see constructions dug deep into the earth, conduits for water, underground passages and air-vents..." The amphitheatre to which Giraldus refers has been thoroughly excavated this century; it stands well outside the fort and is immensely impressive. It is said to have seated six thousand spectators; it was most likely used for military exercises and parades, though it cannot be ruled out that occasionally the hearts of off-duty soldiers were gladdened by the sight of gladiatorial combats. Some time in the middle of the third century, sixty or seventy years before the Roman Empire embraced Christianity, two Roman soldiers stationed in Caerleon, were put to death for their Christian faith. These early martyrs were called Aaron and Julius; their martyrdom is confirmed by Giraldus, who added the information that in later years two churches in Caerleon were dedicated to their memory.

A Roman posting to Segontium (G.R. 485624) can hardly have been popular with the troops; it is situated half a mile south of Caernarfon and a hundred and fifty feet above the shore in a bleak and exposed position. Segontium was at the end of the road. It was an auxiliary fort, built to accommodate a thousand men, its purpose to maintain the Roman peace in Anglesey and in the Llŷn Peninsula. The original fort was put up by Agricola's men in 78 and covers five and a half acres; its wooden buildings were protected by a rampart five feet high, on the top of which was fixed a wooden palisade. Surrounding the fort was a pair of ditches. This lonely Roman outpost was in use on and off throughout the occupation. There is no archaeological evidence that any provision was made for the entertainment or relaxation of Roman soldiers, when off duty, unless the comfort afforded by religion may be placed in that category. In the little museum on the site is an altar to Minerva, dug up in the fort, and in 1959 a temple dedicated to Mithras was excavated. From Segontium a Roman road ran south to another auxiliary fort in an even lonelier situation, that of Tomen y Mur.

Five miles south of Ffestiniog and one mile east of the Trawsfynydd power station the patient and the painstaking student will find the traces in the bleak moorland of the most remote auxiliary fort in Roman Britain. Built on Agricola's orders shortly after 78 Tomen y Mur (G.R. 706386) was linked by road with Segontium to the north-west, to Caerhun to the north and to Brithdir to the south. The original fort was made of wood and turves but when it was reduced in size some years later a stone wall marked the new rampart. Today the aeroplane sees more of the fort than does the walker but even so the outlines are reasonably clear. Inside the fort is a mound whose purpose is puzzling until it is realised that the Normans passed that way a thousand years later and chose the site of the west gate of the Roman fort for the erection of a motte and bailey, which is commemorated in the Welsh name Tomen y Mur, the Mound on the Wall. Near the fort may be seen a flat area which had been artificially levelled to serve as a parade ground, and away to the north-east the remains of an amphitheatre are visible. Tomen y Mur is believed to have been the only auxiliary fort that was allowed the luxury of such an amenity, which surely shows that even the hardheaded Romans recognised the need for some compensation to be given to those soldiers unlucky enough to have been posted to that outpost.

The contrast today between a North Sea oil rig and a Cotswold village can hardly be greater than that between Tomen y Mur and Caer-went. Caer-went, or Venta Silurum as the Romans knew it (G.R. 469905) is well worth a visit: in addition to being visually exciting, it reveals the other side of Roman occupation policy. It was as though the Romans wanted to show the conquered Silures the benefits to be derived from cooperating with them. Venta Silurum became not only the place which Roman soldiers wanted to visit, when on leave from duties with the legion in Caerleon, but also the tribal capital of the Silures to which the leading men of the Silures were invited. Employment, houses and entertainment were all available for their use and enjoyment. The town covered forty-four acres and offered most of the amenities of a small Romano-British town in the Civil Zone, public baths, a forum, shops and a small amphitheatre. The walls that surrounded the town still stand, in places reaching a height of fifteen feet. The modern village of Caer-went, which is all part and parcel of Venta Silurum, enjoys an enviable position, pleasantly situated as it is, close to modern roads but quite screened from them.

Roman withdrawal

The Romans withdrew from Wales shortly before the end of the fourth century A.D.; such a long period of occupation inevitably left its mark on the conquered population, even though Roman influence in Wales was considerably less than in the Civil Zone, further east in Britain. In Wales the most obvious proof of the Roman presence lay in the Latin words that crept into common Celtic usage, words to do with practical matters in which Roman soldiers excelled, to do with fighting and building. Rather more tenuous was the effect Roman military might had in helping to unify those Celtic tribes who had had the courage to stand up against them. That in after years, when new threats to the Celtic home lands were forthcoming from other quarters, the Silures and the Ordovices were able to take the lead and organise resistance may at least in part be attributed to their earlier reputation gained when they had dared to oppose the Roman invader.

Finally it must be put on record that Christianity first came to Wales in the ranks of Roman soldiers. Mention has already been made to two Roman soldiers dying for their Christian faith in Caerleon *(Caerllion)*, but after Constantine, who had been proclaimed Emperor in York, accepted Christianity in about 314, Christianity became the leading religion in the empire, so that some knowledge of it in all probability will have been passed on to those Celts, who had contact with their Roman masters in various forts and mining settlements in Wales. Whether or not Christianity survived the Roman withdrawal from Wales at the end of that century will be considered in due course.

Segontium: south of Caernarfon. On this small but well-kept site is a museum, amongst whose many exhibits is the illustrated altar, dedicated to Minerva.

B. ROMAN REMAINS IN THE TWENTIETH CENTURY

Segontium, Tomen y Mur, Caerleon *(Caerllion)* and Caer-went were all dealt with in the last chapter, the two latter places being the most important Roman settlements in Wales. Nothing further here will be said about these four sites except to draw the reader's attention to a fourth century pewter bowl which was dug up at Caer-went and is now on view in the museum at Newport *(Casnewydd)*, Gwent. It is the oldest surviving Christian artefact in Wales.

Eight places will be described in this chapter, stretching from Anglesey to the south coast of Glamorgan. Where the A5 ends its long journey is the town of Holyhead, above whose harbour can be seen the medieval parish church of St Cybi. This harbour was of considerable importance to the Romans as it afforded a safe anchorage for those Roman ships whose responsibility it was to patrol the Irish Sea. In addition the copper mined in north-east Anglesey will have been exported from Holyhead. By the beginning of the fourth century A.D. Roman occupation problems in Britain had begun to multiply as invaders threatened from several different directions. Hence from about 300 A.D. forts were constructed at many points along Britain's long and exposed shore line. One was built at Holyhead on the headland, where now the church looks across the harbour. This fort, known as Caergybi (G.R. 246827), enclosed the land now occupied by the church and churchyard; it was only a small fort, hardly amounting to an acre in extent, but it gave adequate protection against possible invasion from the sea. Its surrounding wall may still be seen, rising in places to about fifteen feet in height; as the

Caer Gybi: One of the three original round corner towers of the Roman fort, which is now an integral part of the churchyard wall, running round the parish church of Holyhead.

Tomen y Mur: The remotest Roman fort in Britain, 5 miles south of Ffestiniog. This fort is now completely overgrown but in the museum at Segontium may be seen inscribed stones taken from Roman buildings that once stood on that bleak moorland.

wall was five feet thick, it is possible to walk with safety along the rampart. Of its four original round corner towers, three have survived.

Caerhun (G.R. 776704), built in the early years of the Roman occupation of Wales as a staging post on the road from Chester (Deva) to Caernarfon (Segontium), stood near the river Conwy four and a half miles up the river from Conwy. The motorist today, moving south from Conwy on the B5106, in search of what remains of Canovium, should make for the parish church because the walls of the churchyard are supported by a Roman rampart. Little remains today beyond the outlines of the walls which are very clear on the south side of the fort. Nevertheless, thanks to a thorough excavation in the 1920's, the story of the fort has been revealed. It is thought to have been built of wood in 75 A.D. and rebuilt in stone about seventy years later; the site of the fort seems to have been chosen with a view to defending the Roman position from any attack from the river, proof of which has been furnished by the discovery of traces of a jetty and a dock. The Roman occupation of Canovium went on until the fourth century, though most of the buildings are believed to have been destroyed in about the year 200.

A short stop four miles west of Bala on the A494 road to Dolgellau that runs alongside the lake will reveal on a spur to the north of the road the ramparts of a small Roman fort. Caer Gai (G.R. 877315) is to be found half a mile north-east of the village of Llanuwchllyn. Only the ramparts on the south-west and south-east sides of the fort are well-preserved, though an entrance gap on the south-west side is also clearly recognisable as such. All the land encompassed by the fort has been completely filled in. During the excavation of the site a shrine was unearthed near the north-east gate, which was dedicated to Hercules, its inscription, now in the safe keeping of the National Museum in Cardiff, indicating that a cavalry regiment from the north of Gaul had been station at Caer Gai, which, it appears, was only in Roman occupation from about 78 A.D. to 130.

Holiday makers, based on Llandrindod Wells in central Wales, who want to take a break from playing golf or bowls, fishing or taking the foul-smelling (though doubtless health

Caerhun: 4½ miles south of Conwy. As in Holyhead, the walls of the Roman fort here have been incorporated into the churchyard walls. The extension of the wall in one of the photographs originally led to the Roman jetty and dock on the west bank of the river Conwy.

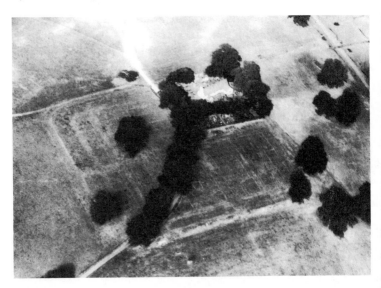

giving!) waters, could do worse than make a short excursion to Castell Collen (G.R. 055628), which lies a mile or so to the north of the spa, off A4081. This large fort was built on high ground between the river Ithon and one of the streams that feed it. As a result of two excavations, one before the First World War, the other after the Second, it is thought that the original fort, a wooden affair, was built between 75 and 78 A.D.; it covered a large area of about five acres and provided accommodation for about a thousand men. It was bounded by a ditch and a wall of turves which was later stregthened by the addition of stones. At the beginning of the third century the area of the fort was halved, the north-west part being abandoned; the strength of the garrison was reduced to five hundred men but the most important of the new buildings were made of stone. Vestigial remains of these stone buildings, more particularly those of the Commandant's house and the headquarters building, have survived but all traces of the wooden barracks in which the soldiers were housed, have long since disappeared. It should be stressed that this excursion is really only for the connoisseur as there is little to be seen though much to be learned from the geographical location and from the finds which are on view in the museum in Temple Street, Llandrindod Wells.

An hour's drive separates Castell Collen from Brecon Gaer, which lies four miles west of Brecon, off the A40, high up above the road, on a strategically important site. The Gaer (G.R, 002297), a cavalry fort with accommodation for five hundred horsemen, was built in this key position about 80 A.D., when the newly-conquered Celtic lands needed to be consolidated. Like other forts it originally consisted of wooden buildings, protected by earthen ramparts, which gave place to stone when they were rebuilt in the following century. There is much more to be seen here than in the forts already described in this chapter; the site was excavated by Sir Mortimer Wheeler in the nineteen twenties.

Today there are on three sides of the fort large sections of well-constructed walls, still in position, rising up to about ten feet in height (the north side has been incorporated in a farm). Three gateways remain of which the southern one is particularly

Caerleon: 2½ miles N.E. of Newport, Gwent. This fort, originally the most important Roman fort in Wales, can still be appreciated thanks to the imaginative care which has been devoted to its preservation and upkeep. Today it is rightly one of the show places of Roman Britain. Illustrated are the amphitheatre, excavated 60 years ago by Sir Mortimer Wheeler, and thought to have held up to 6000 spectators, and the guardroom, adjoining the barrack block. Today's impressive museum is worthy of the headquarters of the 2nd Augustan Legion.

well-preserved with substantial parts of the guardroom walls still standing both sides of the gate. An unusual feature in the Gaer was the presence inside the fort of a bath-house, which normally was built outside the walls. Also of interest is the fact that there is strong evidence that there was a large civilian settlement established outside the north gate. The Gaer was continuously occupied until about 200 when it appears to have been evacuated only to be brought back into use again a hundred years later.

Eight miles west of the Gaer, on the old Roman road that runs from Trecastle *(Trecastell)* to Llandovery *(Llanymddyfri)*, are to be found vestigial remains of two marching camps. There is little to be seen here except earthen ramparts and ditches but to the inner eye of imagination these so-called marching camps (of which there are sixteen surviving sites in Wales and the Marches) make a strong appeal because these camps date from the very earliest years of Roman campaigning against the Celtic lands. Most of these camps were abandoned even before the year 80, by which time organised opposition to the advance of Roman arms had come to an end. Here at Y Pigwyn (G.R. 828313) were two such camps, the smaller of the two being built a few years later than the larger one, within the same perimeter. A whole legion with its auxiliary troops could be quartered there, but only for a short time, indeed sometimes only for one night. They were transit camps with a difference as the front-line troops may have been detailed, immediately on arrival, to dig themselves adequate defences for protection for the ensuing night. Stoutly-built forts in later years, like that at the Gaer, were only made possible by the successful efforts of these units of Roman infantry who made good use of the Spartan facilities afforded by Y Pigwyn and other such marching camps.

Halfway along the A482, which runs in a south-easterly direction from Lampeter *(Llanbedr Pont Steffan)* towards Llandovery, is the strangely-named village of Pumsaint (the five saints referred to in the name were, according to tradition, quintuplets, all of whom became holy men). Half a mile from here the Romans mined gold at Dolau Cothi (G.R. 665405); details of the mines can be found in a pamphlet available in the village inn, where also advice should be sought to help visitors to

Caer-went: 5 miles S.W. of Chepstow. Illustrated is the south wall, which is part of one of the best-preserved sections of Roman walling in Britain. The modern village was built on the site of the Roman market town. Further visits are recommended to the local parish church, which houses 2 inscribed stones, and to the museum in Newport, where Caer-went objects are on exhibition.

find their way about in this difficult terrain. The precious metal was obtained partly by opencast methods and partly by tunnelling into shallow galleries — the entrances to some of these tunnels are still clearly visible but, as mining has gone on in the neighbourhood on a number of occasions since Roman times local enquiries are recommended; caution is also stressed as some of the galleries are too dangerous to explore. Excavation in recent years has greatly increased our knowledge of Roman mining methods here; for instance, traces have been discovered of an aqueduct running up-country for more than ten miles, providing water which is essential for smelting. On display in the National Museum in Cardiff *(Caerdydd)* is part of a Roman water-wheel taken from this economically important site, which, though organised by civilian engineers, was certainly supervised and controlled by units of the Roman army.

On the coast of south Glamorgan, well to the west of Cardiff and south of Cowbridge *(Y Bont-faen)* is a place, well-steeped in early history, Llanilltud Fawr *(Llantwit Major)* (G.R. 959700). On a nearby headland men of the Iron Age protected themselves with a promontory fort. To this district in later days the Romans came and settled, developing over the years a large complex of farm buildings, based on a villa, erected in about 150. The original farm, built in wood, probably consisted of domestic structures built round two sides of a double courtyard, complete with the full array of bath-houses that the Romans always insisted on. To this were later added many barns and workshops. In about 300 there was a wholesale rebuilding of the farm in stone; in this transformation four mosaic floors were laid and several rooms were decorated with painted plaster. Halfway through this fourth century a barbarian raid, presumably form the sea, took place which wrought great havoc in the villa, in one part of which archaeologists discovered the mangled skeletons of many men and horses. Whether the farm continued to function after this disaster is open to doubt. It is necessary here briefly to anticipate events to be dealt with in the next chapter, because tradition has it that Illtud, one of the founding fathers of Christianity in Wales, landed hereabouts from Brittany towards the end of the fifth century and actually lived in the Roman villa, at the same time giving his name to the place, Llanilltud later to be corrupted to Llantwit. Whether or not there is any truth underlying this tradition, what is certain is that there was only a short lapse of time between the end of the Roman occupation of the district and early Christian settlement.

Between Llanilltud Fawr and Cardiff evidence has accumulated of two further Roman villas: excavation at one of the sites, at Whitton (G.R. 081713) revealed traces of Roman farm buildings, erected on an Iron Age settlement, while the other villa, which is much nearer Cardiff, at Ely (G.R. 147762) is thought to have concerned itself with the smelting of iron. On into the centre of Cardiff, where the mighty castle looms up, a massive structure, mostly rebuilt in the nineteenth century, but securely based on Roman foundations. Round the corner from the castle in the splendid array of civic buildings stands out the National Museum of Wales, which is rightly renowned for its collection of prehistoric, Roman and early Christian exhibits, along with artefacts from later periods. The other Roman museums in Wales are virtually site museums, as at Caerleon, Newport (for Caer-went), Brecon (Y Gaer), Llandrindod Wells (for Castell Collen), and Caernarfon (Segontium).

THE CELTIC CHURCH

PENRHOS LLUGWY

PENMON

LLAN-RHOS

LLANFAELOG

LLANSADWRN

ABERFFRAW

LLANBADWALADR

CLYNNOG FAWR

LLYSTYN-GWYN

WHITFORD

HOLYWELL

BANGOR IS-COED

TREFLYS

PENMACHNO

LLANAELHAEARN

LLANGWNNADL

LLANFECHAIN

LLANGIAN

BARDSEY
(YNYS ENLLI)

LLANERFYL

LLANAFAN FAWR

LLANDDEWIBREFI

PEN BRYN

FFYNNON GYBI

CARDIGAN

ST. DOGMAEL'S

LLANDYSUL

TRALLWNG

LLANSBYDDID

NEVERN

LLANFIHANGEL
-AR-ARTH

LLAN-GORS

MESUR-Y-DORTH

DEFYNNOG

CWM DU

ST. DAVID'S

BRAWDY

CARMARTHEN

MAEN MADOG

PARTRISHOW

CARDIFF

LLANILLTUD FAWR

THE CELTIC CHURCH

A. THE AGE OF THE SAINTS

The collapse of Britain

At the beginning of the fifth century in Britain the clock was well and truly put back; the Celts, who inhabited all southern Britain, were left by the departing Roman armies to fend for themselves. Before long, unarmed, untrained and unprotected, they had to face up to attacks from many quarters, from Jutes and Angles and Saxons, and from Picts and Scots. Very little is known for certain about these dark and dismal days of transition in the fifth century and what little we do know is mostly derived from the sole surviving contemporary source, Gildas, a monk, who had been educated at Llanilltud Fawr, of which distinguished seminary more will be said later. As Gildas died in the second half of the sixth century, what he wrote down must either have been hearsay or the recollections of men who in their old age reminisced for the benefit of the young monk from Wales. From Gildas' book, *The Downfall of Britain* it would be safer to gather impressions rather than facts. Out of the thick mist that obscured most of this fifth century there occasionally appeared in outline the dim figure of Vortigern, who made himself leader of the Celts. Much has been written about him but little is known beyond the fact that in the middle of the century he invited Angle and Saxon mercenaries from across the North Sea to come to Britain in order to help him to defend his lands, probably against the Picts. Hengist and Horsa, the Anglo-Saxon leaders, accepted the invitation, rendered the necessary assistance and elected to stay on, and so renewed the foreign occupation of Britain. Of the one and only Arthur, whose adventures were set in this same century, nothing factual may be recounted. Gildas, not the most reliable of chroniclers, failed to mention him, either through ignorance of his existence or, as one tradition insists, because Arthur had killed his brother.

By the year 500 most of Britain was in a state of turmoil and disarray, with Angles, Saxons, Jutes and the men from the north challenging the Celtic Britons for a share in the overlordship of the country. Wales alone at this time stood as yet unmolested by these invaders and indeed earned the distinction of being the only part of the former Roman Empire in the west to escape capture by marauders. All the same there was a grim struggle going on in Wales for survival at this time when there was no central authority. The most significant development occurred when there came down from Strathclyde, in southern Scotland, a Romanised Celt, called Cunedda, who in the early years of this fifth century settled in Anglesey, from which island he drove out Irish immigrants who had lived there for several decades. This Christian Cunedda ruled from Aberffraw on the west coast of Anglesey and there founded a dynasty whose descendants were to serve Wales faithfully and well for more than eight hundred years.

While it is true that there is no proof that Christianity survived in Wales after the withdrawal of the Romans, the fifth century, despite the darkness that fell upon the rest of Britain, which reverted to paganism, witnessed the rapid spread of Christianity in the far west. Nevertheless it is as well to regard this as the return of Christianity to Wales rather than to see it as surviving from Roman days. Had Christianity really managed to hang on after the Romans' departure, then surely traces of it would have been found in the south-east of the country where it was known to have been practised by the Romans, whereas in fact the record does not bear this out.

The first missionaries

The surprisingly speedy expansion of Christianity in Wales in the fifth century at a time when it was abandoned altogether further east in Britain, was above all due to energetic Celtic missionaries coming by sea from western parts of Gaul, probably Brittany. The greatest authority on early Christian tombstones in Wales, Dr. Nash-Williams, draws our attention to the fact that the earliest memorial stones were all inscribed in exactly the same way as those found in western Gaul. He further noted that while there are many of these remarkable Christian memorial stones in Wales, there are none in the south-east, which was the centre of Christianity when the Romans ruled from Caerleon. In addition to these Christian missionaries sailing along the western sea-routes, Irish Christians were at the same time settling in Anglesey and in coastal areas of Wales further south. The archaeological proof of this Irish colonisation is strong, because the Irish Christians had devised a special kind of script for their memorial inscriptions, known as Ogham. Of the very many memorial inscriptions of the fifth and sixth centuries that still survive in Wales some are in Latin, some are in Ogham, and fortunately some are in both. Such a stone, still to be seen in the nave of the church at Nevern (*Nyfer*), in Dyfed, which carries both scripts, enabled scholars to decipher the secrets of Ogham, which consists of a series of notches cut into the edges of the memorial stones; there are several of these fascinating stones, bearing both scripts, on exhibition at the National Museum in Cardiff. Details of these Christian memorial stones, which are still in situ, will be given in the next chapter.

A third possible factor which may have helped the development of Christianity in Wales was the immigration in the early years of the fifth century of Christian refugees from areas further east in Britain, who sought the security of the Welsh hills when the withdrawal of the Roman army left them unprotected. In addition there is good reason to believe that close contact was established between the Celtic immigrants from Gaul and the colonists from Ireland, communication between the various parts of Wales being facilitated by the excellent Roman roads. This cultural contact, which could have helped in later years to unify the Welsh, was fractured when Cunedda and his successors extended their rule from Anglesey to north and central Wales, to the extreme discomfiture of the Irish settlers. It was into this Wales that there came towards the end of this confused fifth century an outstanding Christian missionary, Illtud.

Illtud

When considering these early Christian missionaries it has to be stressed that hard facts are difficult to come by; little was written down for many centuries and when eventually learned monks put on record what they had heard, wishful thinking has to be allowed for. Nevertheless Illtud was certainly one of the founding fathers of the Christian church in Wales; it seems very likely that he hailed from Brittany, from whence he sailed to south Wales towards the end of the fifth century, landing on the south coast of Glamorgan at a spot south of the modern Cowbridge, a spot which had previously been inhabited both by men of the Iron Age and by the Romans. A mile from there Illtud established a monastic college which in the course of time achieved an outstanding reputation for scholarship. This place is now known as Llantwit Major, which is a partial anglicisation of the original Llanilltud Fawr. From this centre of devotion and learning men went forth spiritually and intellectually equipped to spread Christianity and to establish in Wales the monastic movement.

A suitable site would be chosen and a wooden cross set up by the missionary monk who then built himself a simple hut. If he succeeded in attracting an audience and keeping it, he would enclose the area with a circular bank of earth. This was the first *llan*, an area set apart for religious purposes. Sometimes these monks actually settled on sites already enclosed by stone walls, the remains of Bronze Age barrows. All this started in the early days of the sixth century at a time when Illtud himself chose to live the life of a hermit, first at Oystermouth on the Gower

Peninsula, and later at Llanhamlach in the Upper Usk valley.

According to Giraldus Cambrensis, who was writing more than six hundred years later, the mare which carried provisions to Illtud in his rural retreat at Llanhamlach, "became gravid after being covered by a stag and gave birth to a creature which could run very fast, its front part being like that of a horse and its haunches resembling those of a deer." Today in this same parish of Llanhamlach, four miles south-east of Brecon, will be found on private ground belonging to Manest Farm, a neolithic long barrow, with the anachronistic name of Tŷ Illtud, the House of Illtud. It appears that anything old was thought to have something to do with this remarkable man. An added curiosity is that on the walls of the forecourt of the tomb there are carvings, which are certainly much later in date than the tomb itself, some of which look remarkably like crosses as though the eager early Christians believed that by scratching crosses on a pagan tomb some sort of posthumous respectability might be conferred upon the dead. Illtud's presence in this part of Wales was clearly felt, as indeed it was also felt further north on the banks of the river Mawddach, above Dolgellau. Tradition has it that Illtud chose this remote region for an early *llan*, which only in later centuries became the spiritual centre of a village, which bore his name, Llanelltud. In Illtud's *llan* were later erected in a circular churchyard a succession of churches, which the Cistercian monks from nearby Cymer Abbey served until its dissolution in the sixteenth century. It is interesting to note that Illtud had a brother, who too was a priest, whose inscribed tombstone has survived. It is now to be seen in the church of the village named after him, Llansadwrn, in Anglesey, four miles west of Beaumaris.

The scene changes to central Wales, where in the Brecon Beacons to the south-west of Brecon there is a patch of hilly moorland that bears his name, Mynydd Illtud. Here at a height of eleven hundred feet, a short distance from the Mountain Centre at Libanus, is a circular churchyard, (the church is Victorian) in which, according to tradition, Illtud lies buried. Half a mile to the east of the churchyard is a Bronze Age burial cairn, which the reader will hardly be surprised to learn is known as Bedd Illtyd,

Illtud's grave! Wherever he was buried, he is thought to have died in 540, the doyen of the missionary movement. As scholar and Christian leader he was outstanding; his great memorial was the seminary he set up at Llanilltud Fawr, which became famous far and wide as a centre of learning, where along with the knowledge of Christianity were inculcated the classics, grammar, rhetoric and philosophy.

Cadog and Dyfrig

Another famous missionary, though of a lesser magnitude than Illtud, whose contemporary and fellow-worker in the field he was, was Cadog; he was the son of Gwynllyw, a very powerful figure in south-east Wales in the early sixth century and something of a villain too, whom Cadog is credited with having converted to Christianity somewhat late in life. So devoted however did his father become to the Christian cause that the cathedral at Newport was dedicated to him under the later Anglo-Norman form of his name, Woolos. The son, whose floruit was in the early years of the sixth century, though his actual dates are unknown, set up a seat of learning in south Glamorgan, at Llancarfan, which is only about five miles east of Illtud's seminary at Llanilltud Fawr. Unfortunately, the actual position of Cadog's school of learning has remained undiscovered, prompting the likely theory that today's church stands on its very site. That it achieved a great reputation for its scholarship cannot be gainsaid, especially it seems in the study of the Classics. Cadog above all became a great authority on the Roman poet Virgil, perhaps fittingly insofar as the astonishing claim was made on his behalf that he was a descendant of Virgil's master, Augustus himself, the first Emperor of Rome! One of the curious scraps of information that have been handed down about Cadog is that every Spring he spent Lent on the island of Steep Holm in the Bristol Channel, to which island Gildas also retreated, when he wrote his history on *The Downfall of Britain*. Cadog's fame must have spread far and wide because there are churches dedicated to him not only in south-west, south-east

Wales and in Anglesey, but also in Scotland, Cornwall and in distant Brittany.

Rather later than Cadog but still in the sixth century, lived a missionary variously known as Dyfrig, Dubricius and Devereux; there is a village in Herefordshire near Kilpeck, named St Devereux, whose parish church is dedicated to St Dubricius! He lived and worked in south-east Wales and over the borders in what is now Herefordshire. The various references to the holy man's life and career suggest the existence of a thin dividing line between fact and fiction. That he actually lived is certain (he founded a monastery in Herefordshire), that he did half the things attributed to him by Geoffrey of Monmouth most unlikely. In this category must be placed Geoffrey's assertion that he crowned King Arthur! Of his status as a Christian missionary however there can be no doubt. He wandered about the country far less than most missionary monks at that time, although there are strong associations with him on Caldey Island; and, when he died in 612, he was considered to be of sufficient consequence to be buried in Bardsey Island, from which resting place his bones were removed five hundred years later and transferred to Llandaf presumably because of the strength of the legend that he had caused the building of the first cathedral in that place.

St David

In the south-west of the country there were three monks in the sixth century whose missionary endeavours stood out, of whom far and away the greatest was St David himself, the other two being Teilo and Padarn. Indeed Teilo and Padarn accompanied St David on a pilgrimage to Rome and Jerusalem. All the sixth and seventh century missionaries are referred to as saints, but in fact all save David were honorary saints as only David was canonised by the church authorities in Rome. Of Teilo's life and achievements only a skeleton outline is possible. He is believed to have founded a monastery at Llandeilo in Carmarthenshire and he is credited with having been the third Bishop of St David's; certainly there are many churches in Wales dedicated to him. There is a curious story in circulation that Teilo's skull was the private property of a well-known family in the Llandeilo district. Until about fifty years ago, so the story goes, pilgrims to that house were offered a drink of water from the skull, in the belief that such water possessed curative properties. Of St Padarn (or Paternus) even less is known than of Teilo. He was born in Wales and spent his life in the south-west and west of the country, founding a monastery which in after years acquired a great reputation at Llanbadarn Fawr, which today is almost a part of Aberystwyth. Though many churches were dedicated to him, he, like his contemporary Teilo, lived in the shadow of St David.

Most famous old churches occupy prominent positions in the landscape where all may see and wonder, but it is not so with the cathedral at St David's. Uninformed visitors, having parked their cars, may at first look about them in vain for the House of David, Tyddewi, until they are directed to the steep slope below whose thirty-nine steps may be seen the cathedral and the splendid remains of the old Bishop's Palace. It was down here where three cathedrals have since stood that David founded his monastery. It is ironical that so little firm fact is known about one whose fame is so great. The explanation seems to be that more than five hundred years were allowed to elapse before his life was written about, and even then the motives of the writer may well have been mixed, because when Rhigyfarch, the son of a Bishop of St David's, set about, at the end of the eleventh century, putting on record the life and achievements of St David, the Norman penetration into southern parts of Wales had become so deep that the continued independence of St David's from the authority of Canterbury was thought to be at risk. Hence it was essential, if Wales was to withstand the Norman pressure, that the greatness of the father of Welsh Christianity had to be emphasised and embellished with every anecdote and legend that the intervening years had provided.

This south-western corner of Wales must have furnished the young David with much food for thought as he saw around him so much evidence of earlier human occupation. Tradition has assigned his birth to a cave less than a mile south of modern St

David's, where may still be seen the ruins of an early church dedicated to his mother Nonna, who is reputed to have given birth to her illustrious son on that very site. Nearby is an ancient well now dedicated to St Mary, and in the field in which the little church stands are several stones still in position that speak of an earlier prehistoric settlement.

St David is believed to have been educated at a monastic establishment at Henfynyw, near Aberaeron in Dyfed, before going back to the land of his birth, where he founded a monastery at Glyn Rhosyn, where St David's Cathedral now stands. It is incorrect to refer to him as Archbishop of St David's, or even as Bishop, because there was as yet no see and no diocese. David all his adult life was Abbot of his monastery, which, despite the lack of stress laid there on scholarship, became even more famous than Illtud's. Here David made his mark, as an ascetic Christian, of gentle disposition, a firm disciplinarian, an able organiser and above all an inspired and persuasive preacher. It is the stuff of legend, true or false, that he drank nothing but water and harnessed his monks to the plough; despite this or because of it, disciples flocked to the monastery.

The stories about him are legion: one concerns an address he is supposed to have given, when a young man, to a synod convened in a remote place in up-country Dyfed, now named after him, Llanddewibrefi. It was said that when David was called upon to speak he did so with such fire and passion that the very ground on which he stood rose up under his feet so that he found himself standing on a mound, proving to the congregation, now grouped below him that he should be recognised as their leader. The story may be apocryphal but that it should have been invented clearly revealed the need felt to justify the way David stood out above his fellow-men.

He died at a great age on March 1st 588; Jan Morris in *The Matter of Wales* quotes his biographer Rhigyfarch as saying that his last sermon, preached shortly before he died, contained these words: "Lords, brothers and sisters, rejoice and hold fast your faith and belief and do the little things that you have heard from and seen in me." Jan Morris added. "A great host of angels filled the town and all manner of delectable music was heard and the sun shone brilliantly, and Jesu Christ took unto himself the soul of David the Saint with great pomp and honour." Fifty Welsh churches have since been dedicated to him, although none of them is to be found in north Wales. He was canonised in 1120 and thereafter became the patron saint of Wales, the anniversary of his death on the first of March becoming the National Day. The church authorities in Rome moreover subsequently decreed that two pilgrimages to St David's should rate as highly as one to Rome itself.

Beuno

All the Celtic saints so far referred to hailed either from south Wales or from Brittany; the last one to be mentioned, however, Beuno, belonged to the north, in which area his contribution was equal in importance to that of David himself in the south. Although some authorities think that he was educated in Gwent, he was born towards the end of the sixth century at Berriew a few miles south of Welshpool, where he spent most of his early years as a monk. A mile from today's picturesque black and white village of Berriew *(Aberriw)* is a Bronze Age standing stone, proudly referred to as Maen Beuno, Beuno's Stone; once again our forebears sought to make an emblem of their pagan past respectable by giving it a Christian connotation. This stone was said to have been the Saint's first pulpit.

Exasperated, it is believed, by the proximity of the hated Saxons across the river Severn, Beuno moved north-west further into Wales, finally settling in the Llŷn Peninsula at Clynnog Fawr, where he received from one of Cunedda's successors a piece of land on which he built a monastery. This monastery was to last for over three hundred years until it was destroyed in a Viking raid. Nearby he consecrated to Christian use an ancient prehistoric well to which in after years generations of local people had recourse when they sought alleviation from their various ailments. For centuries it became the custom for the sick, after being bathed in the well, to be carried back to the churchyard where they were placed on a pile of straw strewn on the saint's tomb, it being fervently believed that a night spent in this wise would guarantee restoration to full health.

Inside today's church, a relatively modern building, dating from the fifteenth century, and built on the site of Beuno's seventh century monastery, is a huge chest, known inevitably as the Chest of Beuno, though undoubtedly medieval. Lambs or calves born with a certain distinguishing mark on their ears were considered the special concern of Beuno; their owners were required to come to the churchyard with their calves and lambs the following Trinity Sunday when they had to pay a fee to their abbot because of the Nod Beuno, Beuno's mark found on their livestock. This money, tradition insisted, was then placed in the chest, which perhaps, not surprisingly, was believed to possess miraculous powers. This custom was observed well into the nineteenth century.

Beuno, it seems, was as potent a force on sea as he was on land. A rock a mile off-shore, is still marked on the Ordnance Survey map as Gored Beuno; from this outcrop Beuno was reputed to bless the fishermen. He was also credited with the ability to walk on water and on one occasion, when returning from a visit to Anglesey, to his great regret dropped into the sea a book of sermons which he was reading. However when he stepped on to dry land near Clynnog, to his great delight he saw his precious book set out to dry on a stone, where it was being guarded by a curlew. The grateful abbot proceeded to bless the curlew, which is why, it is fondly believed by some, it is still so difficult to find a curlew's nest!

When he died in 642, he was buried in his cell over which in time a chapel was erected, still known as Beuno's chapel, which is linked to the tower of St Beuno's church by a stone-roofed passage. Of all the many legends that have crystallised around the name of Beuno, perhaps the best known as well as being the most bizarre concerned the strange adventure that befell his niece, Winifred, who in her youth was one day waylaid. As she stoutly and successfully resisted the threatened rape, her frustrated attacker drew his sword and cut off her head. St Winifred's Well at Holywell *(Treffynnon)* marks the spot where her severed head as it touched the ground, caused a great spring of water to gush forth. Happily her revered uncle miraculously appeared and restored the head to Winifred's torso, thus enabling her for many years thereafter to serve the church as Abbess of Gwytherin. Many indeed are the churches in north Wales dedicated to Beuno, especially in the Llŷn Peninsula and in Anglesey. Rightly is he regarded as the patron saint of North Wales.

Christian wells and memorial stones

Throughout the fifth and sixth centuries Christian monks like David, Illtud, Cadog, Dyfrig, Padarn and Beuno and a host of lesser-known missionaries between them succeeded in Christianising most of Wales at a time, be it remembered, when the rest of southern Britain had reverted to pagan ways. In all simple societies water supplies were of prime importance; as prehistoric settlement was widespread in Wales, a great many sources of water had been discovered. Early men generally came to identify springs and wells with the supernatural beings, which were believed to live in the water. Hence small offerings were dropped into the wells to ensure a continuing supply of water from the placated deities. Christian missionaries when they found old wells, tended to sanctify them and then turn them into healing wells, which were often associated with the same saints to whom the nearest churches were dedicated. Pagan Celtic peasants who, it is presumed, had always made their offerings to the wells, were after conversion encouraged to continue the practice, especially when their ailments were sometimes seen to disappear after treatment in the wells, where, after Christian sanctification, prayers were offered and blessings pronounced.

Francis Jones in his authoritative *The Holy Wells of Wales* cites over a hundred examples of pre-Christian wells in the neighbourhood of which Christian churches were built. Such wells then received Christian dedications. This Christian well-cult, which must have helped greatly in winning over the pagan Celts to Christianity, was often associated too with pagan, prehistoric burial places. Seeing that prehistoric men chose to settle on sites near convenient water supplies, many a ruined cromlech and barrow were still visible often in the vicinity of wells in the fifth and sixth centuries. Over sixty instances are known in Wales of prehistoric megaliths being found near sanctified pre-Christian wells; these too were often sanctified by early Celtic missionaries so that these prehistoric stones could also become a part of the healing process emanating from the holy wells.

Instances of this conversion to Christian use of prehistoric monuments may be seen at St Non's chapel, near St David's, where the chapel ruins stand in a prehistoric stone circle, close to a pre-Christian well, now the Holy Well of St Mary; at Nevern, further north up the same coast, where near the church is a well, Ffynnon Garreg, sited near a prehistoric mound, Bedd Samson; at Llangybi, between Lampeter and Tregaron, near whose parish church is a well Ffynnon Gybi, not far from Llech Gybi, a cromlech, where the sick used to be taken to sleep after being dipped in the healing well; and finally at Llanfechain, north-west of Welshpool, where in the round churchyard that surrounds St Garmon's church is a Bronze Age mound, known as Garmon's Mound, three hundred yards from which is St Garmon's Well. All in all, during the rightly-named Age of the Saints the Christian church took over lock, stock and barrel the outstanding features of those pre-Christian religious ceremonies that had to do with wells and megaliths.

Besides a remote track high up in the Brecon Beacons, in the garden of a private house in the Llŷn Peninsula, built into a farmyard wall near the road from Pwllheli to Caernarfon, in the middle of a field above the sea north of Cardigan and in churches and churchyards the length and breadth of Wales will be found the gravestones of early Christians, converted by these Celtic missionaries in the fifth, sixth and early seventh centuries. In all, well over a hundred such monuments have survived; the inscriptions, either in Latin or in Ogham, or in both, generally consist of the name of the dead person and of his or her father; sometimes an inscription is preceded by *HIC IACIT*, the more grammatical *HIC IACET* being rare, and often the words *IN PACE* have been added. Many stones have also carved on them some form of the Christian cross. The Chi-Rho monogram, that rarest of all Christian emblems, occurs twice on Welsh tombstones; both were dug up outside but are now propped up inside the churches of Treflys, in the parish of Cricieth, and of Penmachno in Gwynedd.

The historic meeting at Aust

Nine years after St David, his great work done, had passed from the scene, the Pope sent to Britain in 597 St Augustine and a party of forty monks, who were charged with the onerous task of converting the Saxon heathen. As the newly-arrived missionaries struggled, not without a measure of success, to overcome the stubborn paganism of the Saxons, they must have been surprised to learn of the strength of the Christian church among the Celts in the west. At any rate in 602 Augustine sought a meeting with representatives of the Celtic Christians. Although he had been commissioned by the Pope to act in a friendly manner towards the Celts and to cooperate with them, he was perturbed to hear that in the two centuries that had elapsed since direct control between Rome and Britain had ceased, practices in this Celtic church had deviated in certain respects from those current in Rome. The main differences were said to concern baptismal rites and the date set aside for the celebration of Easter, though in all probability Augustine may well have been offended by the affront to his authority implicit in the independent attitude of the Celtic Christians.

Our knowledge of what actually went on at this historic meeting between Augustine and the leaders of the Celts relies entirely on the account given by Bede, who lived nearly a century later and who was very much biassed against the Celtic Christians, whom he regarded as the enemies of his church. The parties met at Aust, where the Romans before them had established a ferry, south of the Bristol Channel, opposite Chepstow. Augustine apparently expressed the hope that there would be full cooperation between the Celtic church and the newly-established church in Canterbury, but that for this to come about the Celts would have to abandon those practices that differed from existing Roman ones. The Celts listened and then asked for an adjournment to enable them to consult those who had sent them. The Celtic emissaries thereupon returned to their base, which was the great monastery at Bangor Is-coed *(Bangor-on-Dee)*, south-east of modern Wrexham. Here, where no fewer than two thousand four hundred monks were housed, they were advised after due discussion and debate to return to Aust and to accept Augustine's proposals on condition that he should behave toward them in what they regarded as a considerate manner, evidence of which would surely be, if the great man should rise to receive them on their approach.

Augustine, little sensing the delicacy of the situation, remained seated and proceeded to repeat his demands concerning baptism and the timing of Easter in such hectoring tones that it became obvious to the Celts that no compromise was possible. Without such full agreement Augustine made it clear that no common effort to convert the pagan Saxons could be attempted. The opportunity passed; the Celts in anger refused the offer and in return Augustine ominously threatened that if they would not be his friends, they would have to take the consequences of being his enemies. The blood-stained sequel to this threat will be described later, but, as a result of this ill-starred conference, the rift between the two branches of the Christian church in Britain gaped ever wider.

Catamanus Stone: On the north wall of the chancel in the parish church of Llangadwaladr, 2 miles east of Aberffraw in Anglesey. This memorial stone, originally in the churchyard, was erected in 625 by Cadwaladr in honour of his grandfather, Cadfan (Catamanus in Latin), whose forebear was Cunedda himself.

Llansadwrn: West of Beaumaris in Anglesey. This stone, formerly in the churchyard, and now in the parish church, commemorates Sadwrn and his wife; Sadwrn, Saturninus in Latin, was the brother of Illtud and died in 530, making this the oldest Christian inscribed stone in Anglesey.

B. SURVIVING CHRISTIAN MEMORIAL STONES AND WELLS

This chapter will be a long one for the most fortunate reason that Wales is blessed with an exceptionally rich heritage of reminders of the early days of Christianity. Most of the Christian memorial stones to be mentioned in this chapter commemorate the lives of Christians who died before Augustine brought back Christianity to the eastern parts of Britain at the end of the sixth century. A tribute must first be paid to the enthusiasm, the thoroughness and the scholarship of Dr. V. E. Nash-Williams, whose book *The Early Christian Monuments of Wales*, published by the University of Wales in 1954, gives a detailed account of all the fifth and early sixth century Christian memorial stones that survived in Wales at the time of writing his book. This invaluable work of reference described every Christian burial stone that bore either an inscription (in Latin or in Ogham or in both) or an incised cross of varying designs. Only a selection of them will be included in this chapter, either because the author has not visited them all or because some of them in the intervening years have either deteriorated to such an extent that the inscriptions are no longer legible or have altogether disappeared or because, in a small minority of cases, some have passed into the careful custodianship of right-minded private individuals, whose anonymity it seems prudent to protect, except in special circumstances.

Rarest of all early Christian monuments in Britain are those that bear, in addition to a Latin inscription, the Chi-Rho symbol, that is the combined first two letters of Christ in Greek, the Chi and the Rho, the Ch and the R. There are twelve in all in Britain,

Penmachno Stones: Penmachno lies 3 miles S.W. of the A5 in Gwynedd, between Betws-y-coed and Pentrefoelas. These 4 stones, now in the parish church, all commemorate early Christian burials in the district. Of the 4 illustrations, particular attention should be paid to the one that bears the Chi-Rho monogram They all date from the 5th or early 6th century. (See pages 88, 90 and 92.)

of which two are to be seen in North Wales, one at Treflys, the other at Penmachno. Only the most committed enthusiasts will find their way to Treflys church (G.R. 532379) which stands alone high up above the Black Rock sands on the south coast of the Llŷn Peninsula. To acquire the key to this church, which is always locked, and necessarily so, recourse has to be had to the Rectory in Cricieth, which is five miles away up narrow and tortuous country lanes. The inscribed stone which was discovered in the church-yard, has found a home inside the church, where it stands against the north wall of the chancel. The actual Chi-Rho is of a transitional type, being halfway between a Chi-Rho proper and a cross; the accompanying inscription indicates that Jaconus, the son of Minus was buried there.

Penmachno is a large village, situated on the B4406, about three miles south-west of the A5 from which it branches off between Betws-y-coed and Pentrefoelas. The village church has provided sanctuary for four inscribed stones, all belonging to the fifth or early sixth centuries. The key is readily available from an address listed in the porch. The stone with the Chi-Rho monogram announces, in very imperfect Latin, that, "Carausius lies here in this pile of stones". This is no longer true as all four stones were taken into the church from various sites outside, one of which was the garden wall of the Eagle Hotel opposite the church, from which it was rescued in 1915! The accompanying photograph gives a good idea of this splendid early Christian monument. Of the other three stones in the church, one, with only a fragment of Latin inscription surviving, was dug up when the previous church was pulled down, another, still having intact five lines of inscription, concerns itself with the burial of a cousin of a magistrate, one Maglos, while the third added to the name of the deceased the valuable fact that Justinus was the consul that year. As Justinus was consul in the year 540, the actual year of this burial is known (see illustration).

All the many simple memorial stones listed by Nash-Williams possessed features that enabled them to be positively identified as Christian. Two, as has been seen, bore the Chi-Rho symbol, many others had crosses of varying types, and a great many carried inscriptions which often gave details of the dead person's

father or indicated some other relationship. Some inscriptions were preceded by *HIC IACIT* (rarely the grammatically more correct Hic Iacet) and some ended with *IN PACE* or often just *PACE*. In making a selection of memorial stones to be visited, as fair a geographical spread as possible has been attempted.

Four stones out of a possible eleven have been selected in the historian's happy hunting ground of Anglesey, of which the first will be found in the chancel of the church at Penrhos Llugwy (G.R. 481859), set on high ground to the south of a minor road which branches off the A5025 little more than a mile north of Llanallgo in the east of the island. The church is locked and no indication is given where a key may be obtained but fortunately the chancel glass is clear so that the inscription which is on the south wall can be seen through the north window, even the *HIC IACIT* being clearly visible. It is thought to date from the middle of the sixth century and commemorates the death of a Christian Irish chief. This is one of several Irish memorial stones in Anglesey belonging to this period; their surviving relatives were soon to be driven south out of the island by the incoming Christian Celts from Strathclyde, who established themselves at Aberffraw in western Anglesey.

After leaving Penrhos Llugwy the motorist or cyclist will find himself on course for the second memorial stone, if he makes for Llanerchymedd in the centre of the island, where he should get on to the B5112, which seven miles further on in a south-westerly direction becomes the A4080 when the road crosses the A5. Two miles further south still on this road a lookout should be kept for a single storey house on the right hand side named Maen Hir (Long Stone). Opposite this house, just inside a boundary wall on the other side of the road, is the burial stone, Llanfaelog (G.R. 356745). It is marked on the O.S. Map as Inscribed Stone. The simple inscription *CUNDEUS HIC IACIT* refers to a Christian burial in the late fifth or early sixth century. As the visitor gazes at this stone in this remote place, he should marvel that a Christian was buried here at least a hundred years before Pope Gregory sent Augustine north on his civilizing mission to Kent.

This same road, the A4080, after passing through the village of

Llanfaelog leads in five miles to Aberffraw itself, where Cunedda made his headquarters when he first came down from Strathclyde. Members of his dynasty, who were to rule Anglesey and Gwynedd for many a century, were buried in a royal burial ground two miles to the east where the village of Llangadwaladr now stands. One of these royal memorials survives, having been moved from the churchyard into the village church, where it is now built into the north wall, providing posterity with the most remarkable of all early Christian memorial stones in the whole of Britain. The church (G.R. 383693) is always locked but the key may be obtained locally, details in the church porch. The stone on which is also carved a Christian cross, bears this inscription: Catamanus Rex Sapientisimus Opiniatisimus Omnium Regum. (Catamanus wisest and most famous of all kings). Catamanus, which is the Latinised form of Cadfan, was a direct descendant of Cunedda. The memorial was put up in 625 by his grandson, Cadwaladr, who was to give his name to the village and his patronage to the church.

The last of the memorial stones to be visited in Anglesey is in the south-eastern corner of the island, Llansadwrn (G.R. 555759), which is north of Menai Bridge and west of Beaumaris. The key to this rather isolated church is available from the farmhouse, which is the nearest building to the church. The stone which was dug up in the churchyard and is now on the north side of the church, is the oldest one in Anglesey, dating from about 530; it commemorates Sadwrn, who was the brother of Illtud himself. The inscription reads: Saturninus se(pultus) (i) acit et sua sa(ncta) coniu(n)x. Pa(x) vobiscum sit. Saturninus (which is the Latin form of Sadwrn), and his saintly wife lie buried here. Peace be with you both.

Moving across the Menai Straits to the mainland of North Wales the next area to be explored in the Llŷn Peninsula, which furnishes four differing types of early Christian memorial stones. First to the resort of Abersoch on the south coast, two miles north-west of which is the village of Llangian (G.R. 295289), whose churchyard contains a remarkable memorial stone, remarkable in so far as it bears the first reference to a doctor in the history of the Principality. Tradition assigns the first church

here to the sixth century, to the early years of which Nash-Williams also ascribes the stone, which is to be found, probably with some difficulty, in the south side of the churchyard, quite near the south door of the church. Thirty years ago it was reported that the top of the stone had been adapted to form a sundial. This top has now been removed but the three holes are still visible in the stone through which the dial was formerly secured. The inscription, which is on the eastern side of the stone, reads *MELI MEDICI FILI MARTINI IACIT*. Dr. Melius, son of Martin, lies here. Patience is required to read the inscription nowadays; in a poor light visitors could be forgiven for thinking that they were looking at a plain stone slab! Time is certainly taking its toll of a unique inscription.

Llangwnnadl church, which is the next place to be looked at, lies about eight miles north-west of Llangian across the peninsula, and quite near the north coast. In very early days the little wooden church here provided a welcome resting place for pilgrims on their way from Clynnog Fawr to Bardsey Island. The church is dedicated to Gwynhoedl, who flourished about 600, having been trained at the famous monastery at Bangor Iscoed. When the present church, a splendid three-aisled building, was being renovated in 1940, an early burial stone was uncovered when the plaster was removed from the south wall. This stone, which some think marked the burial place of the patron saint of the church, carries no inscription but has incised on it a ringed cross, that is a cross within a circle. Faint traces of the original red paint on the cross are still visible.

Further evidence of early Christian activity in the peninsula is provided by the church and churchyard at Llanaelhaearn, a large village situated under the brooding presence of Tre'r Ceiri, where people of the Iron Age had settled many centuries previously. The village is on the B4417, about six miles north-east of Nefyn and about the same distance north of Pwllheli. The church is locked but, when last visited, the key was obtainable from No 6, a house just opposite the church. A late fifth or early sixth century inscribed stone, which was dug up in a field near the church, fittingly known as Gardd-y-Sant, the Garden of the Saints, was taken into the church and set into the

Maen Madog: This inscribed stone marks an early Christian burial at the side of the Roman road, Sarn Helen, 1400 feet above sea level. Sarn Helen today is a narrow gated track, off the country road, which leads from Heol Senni in south Powys to Ystradfellte, which lies about a mile and a half to the south of the stone.

west wall. Its Latin inscription, *ALIORTUS ELMETIACO HIC IACET*, informs the reader that the dead man belonged to a far distant Celtic province, Elmet, in what is now eastern Yorkshire. Whether Aliortus died on a visit or in retirement in the district is a matter for surmise. A curiosity aboyut the inscription is the grammatically correct spelling of *IACET*. Just inside the churchyard gate on the right hand side, is a second stone, probably still in its original position; the brief surviving inscription indicates that the dead man's name was probably Melitus.

Llystyn Gwyn (G.R. 482455) is for the connoisseur rather than for the photographer. Seven miles along the busy A487, which runs from Porthmadog to Caernarfon, there is a small layby on the left hand side of the road. Park the car here and look eastwards, where half a mile up a steep farm track is a hill farm, Llystyn Gwyn. In the farmyard is a sixth century memorial stone with Ogham script along the edge and Latin on its face. Nash-Williams noted that it marked the grave of Icorix, the son of Potentinus. Today the Latin is well-nigh indecipherable, though the Ogham has more successfully withstood the onslaught of the weather. The stone itself is clearly identifiable as it has been properly built into the wall of the farmyard under a lintel of blue slate. One can but muse upon what sort of a man this Icorix was and how he came to be commemorated on this bleak and windswept hill.

By way of contrast the next stone to be tracked down is secure in the busy church of St. Mary at Llanrhos (G.R. 793803), a suburb of Llandudno. This stone is clearly treasured as it has been excellently mounted. The priest, Sanctinus, we are told, rests here in peace. The date of the burial was probably early in the sixth century. An accompanying brass plate states the known facts: "This stone stood from time immemorial at Tyddyn Holland, a cottage between Bodafon and Little Orme's Head, about 2187 yards in a straight line from this church and was removed to this place A.D. 1908." The key to the church may be obtained from the vicarage, which is down the road in the direction of Llandudno.

Last of the stones to be looked at in North Wales is in the

Y Trallwng: In Powys, north of the A40 between Brecon and Sennybridge. This late 5th century or early 6th century stone, remembering Cunocennius in Latin and in Ogham, is fixed to the south wall of the nave of St David's church. Until the old church was restored, and virtually rebuilt in 1861, it acted as a lintel in a window of the church.

St Dogmaels: A large village 1 mile south of Cardigan. In the parish church is a well-preserved stone, inscribed in Latin and Ogham, honouring the memory of one Sagranus. This Ogham inscription in St Dogmaels was the first to be successfully deciphered by scholars, thus ensuring the future translation of all Ogham inscriptions.

church at Whitford, between Prestatyn and Holywell (G.R. 147782). Here at the west end of the nave is a sixth century stone which originally stood in Plas-yn-Rhos farm, near Caerwys. The inscription runs thus. *HIC IACIT MULIER BONA NOBILIS.* Here lies Bona, the wife of Nobilis.

Two places are recommended for visits in mid-Wales before the richly rewarding area south and west of Brecon is reached. The first of these is Llanerfyl (G.R. 035096) which is a village in Powys, on the Welshpool to Dolgellau road beyond Llanfair Caereinion. Here in a round churchyard high above the road is an immense and ancient yew tree beneath whose sprawling branches a very early Christian tombstone was discovered, belonging to the late fifth or early sixth century. This stone, which is today housed inside the church at the back of the nave, commemorates the death of a thirteen-year old girl, Rustece, daughter of one, Paterninus. The accompanying words *IN PACE*, which first appeared on memorial inscriptions in the fourth century, indicate that Rustece was a Christian.

The other place in central Wales is the parish church of Llanafan Fawr in Powys (G.R. 969558), situated on the B4358, south-west of Newbridge-on-Wye. The church itself, the key to which may be obtained from the Red Lion Inn opposite, was rebuilt a hundred years ago, when it was greatly reduced in size. It stands in an immense round churchyard, the north side of which has received no burials. The site, which is probably a prehistoric one, the church itself being built on top of a mound which could well have been a round barrow, is of special interest to prehistorians as the restored porch contains three unusual stones mortared into its east wall, one of which is spiral, inviting comparison with the spirally decorated stones at Barclodiad-y-Gawres in Anglesey. Evidence of early Christian activity here, apart from the tradition that St Afan the patron saint is buried in the churchyard, is provided by a broken memorial stone, now lying on its side on the floor of the chancel. Although it bears no inscription, there is incised on it a ringed cross, which is thought to suggest the seventh century.

The district around Brecon is rich in early Christian survivals. In the triangle contained by the A470, the A40 and the A479,

Nevern: Inscribed stone: Nevern is halfway between Cardigan and Fishguard, in Dyfed.

Nevern has two inscribed stones, one inside the church, the other, illustrated here, in the churchyard near the south door, its indented Ogham marks on the western edge being clearly visible.

south-east of Brecon, there is evidence of early Christian burial on three sites. At the side of the road at Scethrog a sixth century stone was discovered, dedicated to Nennius, son of Victorinus. This is now in the safe keeping of the museum in Brecon. The other sites in this triangle are the parish churches of Llan-gors and Cwm Du. St Paulinus' Church, Llan-gors (G.R. 135275), which lies on the B4560, just north of the lake of the same name, was heavily restored in the nineteenth century but has custody of three early Christian stones. When last visited these stones were found to have been moved from their usual places in the church to enable some internal repair work to be carried out. In consequence it was not possible to make a proper inspection of these treasures, the most important and earliest of which is a seventh century specimen which has a ringed cross carved on its face.

St Michael's Church, Cwm Du (G.R. 181238) is a few miles to the south-east, on the A479 road between Talgarth and Abergavenny. This is a fine old church, standing up impressively as befits a Michael dedication, in a very large round churchyard, the periphery of which is marked by more than twenty-five yew trees. There are two early Christian stones here; one is lodged in the porch adjoining the priest's door, a Latin Cross adorning a late sixth or early seventh century pillar stone, while the other has been built into a southern buttress halfway between the south porch and the priest's entrance. This sixth century memorial slab is inscribed with *CATACUS HIC IACIT FILIUS TEGERNACUS*; apparently this Catacus stone was found in a field about a mile from the church.

In the space of ten miles or so westwards of Brecon, on or near the A40, are to be found three churches, all privileged to have within their precincts evidence of early Christian associations. The nearest to Brecon, just three miles to the west of it, on the A40 is the church at Llansbyddyd (G.R. 012282), which is dedicatd to Cadog, the early sixth century contemporary of Illtud. The present church is basically fourteenth century, much restored in mid-Victorian times, but it stands in a circular churchyard whose boundaries are marked by nine or ten ancient yew trees. On the north side of this churchyard almost hidden in

St Non's Chapel, near St Davids: According to tradition, St Non gave birth to St David in the field seen in this general view; the Chapel was built to commemorate the historic event. In the foreground of the picture may be seen a low standing stone, which is one of a number to be found in the field, suggesting a Bronze Age settlement, a theory reinforced by the presence nearby of a well, which was later sanctified and dedicated to St Mary.
The second illustration is of the ruined interior of the chapel, against the wall of which may be seen a 7th c. gravestone, which was dug up in the surrounding field.

a group of mostly untended nineteenth century graves is a sixth century memorial stone; although it bears no inscription to identify the dead, the slab is unusually decorated, having two ringed crosses, linked by a carved "stem". The top cross in addition has four small crosses surrounding it.

Y Trallwng is rather difficult to find. Continue on the A40 in a westerly direction for about another mile and a half, then turn right on to a minor road which soon crosses the river Usk. Half a mile beyond the bridge turn left and the hamlet of Y Trallwng lies about a mile along this narrow country road. The church (G.R. 965297), dedicated to St David, was saved from the ravages of time in 1861 when the present building took the place of its crumbling predecessor. In the course of this wholesale restoration a late fifth or early sixth century memorial stone was uncovered in a window, where it acted as a lintel. It is now clamped to the south wall of the nave just inside the church door. There is a double inscription, in Latin and in Ogham, commemorating one Cunocennius. The ringed cross at the top of the slab is thought to have been added a century or so after the burial.

From Y Trallwng either return to the A40 by the outward route or continue westwards until a lefthand turning leads once more to the A40. In either case leave the A40 at Sennybridge, turning left on to the A4067. Half a mile along this road is the village of Defynnog. The church (G.R. 925279), dedicated to Cynog, is on the right hand side, immediately south of a hotel, and just before the road bifurcates. The mostly fourteenth century church is on the site of a very early foundation indeed, possibly dating back even to the late fifth or early sixth century, to which period belongs the memorial stone, which is now propped up against the west side of the porch. The Latin inscription names the dead man as Rugnatio, the son of Vendonus. Above the inscription are two crosses, one ringed and the upper resembling a St Andrew design. Both these crosses were thought by Nash-Williams to have been added after the original burial.

For the last excursion in Powys a considerable diversion will be necessary, which most of those who make the effort will think well worthwhile. From Defynnog take the left hand fork on to

St Seiriol's Well, Penmon: Penmon is where the road ends on the most easterly point of Anglesey. St Seiriol was the brother of Cynlas, who in the 6th c. built the first church at Penmon; here in a hut, near the well lived Seiriol, preaching and healing, and baptising his converts in the well.

the A4215. After about a mile turn right on to a minor road, finger-posted Heol Senni. Just before the village of that name is reached turn left and after a few hundred yards turn right again, as though going to Ystrafellte. This road takes to the hills, winding upwards via a hairpin bend, less than a mile past which will be seen, on the left hand side, not far from the road, a tall stone, Maen Llia. This ancient and interesting stone is worth a brief visit, but it has no known Christian connection. Continue on the mountain road for another one and a half miles, when a gated track branches off on the right. This is the ancient trackway Sarn Helen. Great care will be needed to identify this gated track. An Ordnance-Survey map is essential. The track itself is quite passable for a reasonably-sized car and leads after about three-quarters of a mile to Maen Madog (G.R. 919158), a stone nearly ten feet high, which stands a few feet away from the left verge of the track. This impressive memorial has an inscription carved on its south face, which reads *DERVAC FILIUS IUST IC IACIT*. Dervacius, the son of Justus, lies here, a silent fifth or early sixth century Christian witness, nearly fourteen hundred feet above sea-level looking out on this bleak moorland.

Llanddewibrefi (G.R. 664554) is an upland village in Dyfed, above the Teifi valley, lying on the B4343, that runs from Tregaron to Lampeter. To this place in reverent pilgrimage come those Welshmen who concern themselves with the life of their patron saint. For a strong tradition insists that St David in 519 actually preached on the very mound on which the present church stands. The sight of the church on the mound prompts the thought that earlier men than St David may also have held this place sacred in prehistoric times. Within the circular walls of the churchyard there survives much to remind today's visitors of early Christian occupation of the site. Built (upside down) into the outside wall of the church is a sixth century stone inscribed in Latin, while another inscribed stone can be seen ouside the east end too. In addition there are four other early memorial stones in the churchyard, probably dating from the seventh to the ninth centuries. All in all Llanddewibrefi is a very special place.

There are so many churches in this part of Wales which possess early inscribed stones that some selection is essential, though

The Virtuous Well, Tryleg: Tryleg, on the west side of the Wye valley in Gwent has already been visited to see Harold's Stones. This well, formerly known as St Anne's Well, lies south of the village and is the best-known ancient well in Gwent.

very invidious. Llanddewibrefi had, through its association with St David, to be an automatic choice. In the end a geographical factor was allowed to decide the issue. Lllanddewibrefi looks down on the river Teifi, which, in the course of its winding passage to the sea, passes through two locations whose parish churches keep a watchful eye on early Christian memorials, Llanfihangel-ar-arth and Llandysul, before rushing on towards the sea at Cardigan. This rather arbitrary choice inevitably eliminates from inspection a number of inscribed stones well worth visiting, amongst which are those on Caldey Island *(Ynys Bŷr)*, and in the churches at Cilgerran, Cynwyl Gaeo, Eglwys Gymyn, Llanboidy *(Llanbeidy)*, Llan-dawg, Llangeler, Llan-saint, Pendine *(Pentywyn)* and Silian.

The church at Llanfihangel-ar-arth stands on a mound in a circular churchyard, suggesting an earlier association with matters of life and death in the Bronze Age. The key to the church may be obtained from the Eagle Inn opposite. The inscribed stone, which used to be propped up outside the church, now has its home in the vestry, south of the chancel. It commemorates in Latin Ulcagnus the son of Senomaglus, who lived towards the end of the fifth century.

Three miles downstream is the busy market town of Llandysul, whose church, dedicated to Tysul, reputedly the cousin of St David, was established here in very early times on the bank of the river Teifi. Among the many features of this impressive church is an inscribed stone, now inserted in the inside wall of the west tower. It is but a fragment of a larger slab which once served as part of a stile that gave access to the churchyard. What remains of this sixth century inscription reads, Velvor Filia Broho. Velvoria, the daughter of Brohomaglus lies here. Another Christian survival here is an ancient altar which now forms part of the stone altar in the Lady Chapel, which the local church guide rightly refers to as, "one of the most important relics in all Wales."

Twenty miles to the west the Teifi is finally swallowed up in the sea at Cardigan. Before moving south down a coast, which is wonderfully rich in historical evidence and which illuminates many different chapters of the human story, a brief excursion northwards is recommended to Penbryn, where at the top of a field not far from the sea, is an inscribed stone, six feet high (G.R. 289514). It is to be found about half a mile south of the church and immediately opposite the Duffryn Bern caravan Park. The inscription is interesting. Corbalengi Iacit Ordovs. The stone of Corbalengus. He lies here, an Ordovician. Though carved in the late fifth or early sixth century the mason saw fit to remember that the dead man was a member of the Ordovicians, a Celtic tribe which the Romans thought they had obliterated before the year 100.

Just over a mile south of Cardigan is the large village of St Dogmael's *(Llandudoch)*. Near the very considerable ruins of St. Mary's Abbey is the parish church (G.R. 164459), whose precincts contain yet another sixth century inscribed memorial stone; this one, which is between six and seven feet high, bears on it inscriptions both in Latin and in Ogham. Commemorated here is Sagranus, the son of Cunotamus. Of added interest is the fact that it was the study of these clearly inscribed stones at St Dogmael's that enabled scholars in 1848 to unravel the secrets of the Ogham alphabet, whose use does not seem to have survived the sixth century.

Cardigan at the mouth of the Teifi was the most southerly part of the territory ruled over by the successors of Cunedda, who, it has already been stated, dispossessed Christian Irish immigrants, who had preceded them in settling in Wales. South of Cardigan, however, the Irish felt safe; hence south of the river Teifi the greatest concentration of the Irish Ogham script is to be found. About ten miles south-west of Cardigan, according to tradition, an Irish monk called Brynach established himself in a secluded well-wooded area under a hill and built himself a church sometime in the sixth century. Today's church at Nevern *(Nyfer)* (G.R. 082401), hidden in a valley and approached through an avenue of yews, is dedicated to him. This church and churchyard is very rich in early Christian associations and will be visited again in a later chapter. In the churchyard near the south door and slightly to the east of it stands a splendid fifth or sixth century memorial stone, commemorating, both in Latin and in Ogham, Vitalianus Emeretus. Inside the church, on a window sill on the south wall of the nave is another inscribed stone, again in both Latin and Ogham, to the memory of Maglicunus the son of Clutorius. This slab was originally found in the wall of the passage that led to the priests' chamber above the nave. There is a third feature in Nevern, which illustrates the importance of the area in early Christian times; about one hundred and thirty yards up a hill to the west of the church towards Frongoch is the Pilgrims' Cross, which is a cross cut into the rock face above a stone recess, where pilgrims knelt in prayer. This hallowed spot is thought to have been a wayside shrine for pilgrims en route from Holywell to St David's.

There are more crosses incised on stones in the Fishguard area further south. At Llanllawer (G.R. 986359), about two miles to the south-east of the town, in the Gwaun valley, a large cross was carved in the sixth century on a gatepost at the entrance to the church, the special reason for which can only be guessed at. Again, at Llanwnda (G.R. 932392), two miles to the north of Fishguard *(Abergwaun)*, east of Strumble Head, a place that in the late eighteenth century enjoyed a few brief days of fame when twelve hundred Frenchmen were prevented from making a successful landing in west Wales, several stones with crosses carved on them have been built into the outside walls of the parish church.

There is one more stone to be viewed with a cross carved on its face; it is situated (G.R. 838306) at the side of the road on the A487, south of Fishguard on the way to St David's, a mile north-east of the village of Croes-goch. Known as Mesur-y-dorth it is a vertical slab of stone set into the wall; on it a rough cross has been carved in a circle, which tradition associates with St David, who is reputed to have caused it to be carved to act as a pattern for a large loaf of bread to be conformed to in a period of shortage! It is probably a memorial stone dug up in the neighbourhood, and resembles a similar stone which is ascribed to the seventh century, now propped up against an inside wall of St Non's chapel, the ruined church beyond St David's, where St Non is alleged to have given birth to St David.

The last church to be visited is quite difficult to find, although it is little more than seven miles east of St David's. It would be as well to look to the heavens for guidance, as the church is near the RAF fighter training station at Brawdy *(Breudeth)*. There is little sign of life in Brawdy except the aerodrome and a farm next to the church (G.R. 858240), whose churchyard is both circular and very large, and in summer much overgrown with brambles. In the porch are three memorial stones, two of which are horizontal and the other vertical. This vertical stone and the smaller of the horizontal ones have Latin inscriptions, while the other one has a message in Ogham. Two of these gravestones have holes in them, suggesting that at some time in their long history they may have been used as gateposts. Inside the church there is a fourth memorial stone, with an incomplete inscription in Latin. All in all visiting Brawdy is rather like finding unexpected signs of life on a desert island!

While most early Christian inscribed memorial stones in Wales are still to be found in churches and churchyards, some of them have been removed for safe custody to museums, especially those that have been discovered at the side of the road, or dug up by the plough. Both Swansea Museum and Margam Abbey Museum of Stones have on exhibition such stones well worth viewing, but the major collections are to be seen in the museums at Brecon, Carmarthen *(Caerfyrddin)* and Cardiff, a visit to Brecon being a necessary complement to visits to those sites in south Powys already described.

Field and farm, as well as churchyard have yielded up six inscribed stones for which the new museum at Carmarthen, formerly the Bishop's Palace, has provided an ideal setting. Lastly a leisurely stay at the National Museum in Cardiff is highly desirable by way of rounding off a study of these early Christian stones. As befits a national museum, it contains inscribed stones from all over the country, from Gwynedd to Dyfed and Glamorgan, all set out to the best possible advantage.

In the last chapter something was said of the importance of wells in the early days of the Christian church in Wales, surviving wells near St David's and near Clynnog Fawr in the Llŷn Peninsula, in particular showing a close connection with St David and St Beuno respectively. Again and again Christian missionaries, who were forced to settle near a suitable supply of water, tended thereafter to bless these wells thus sanctified in Wales in the fifth, sixth and seventh centuries, some of which had already been in use in pagan times. Of the very many wells, a few well-known examples that are still clearly recognisable as wells will here be described.

Many of these old wells are no longer shown even on Ordnance Survey maps, though where they are marked in gothic type indicating their antiquity, an investigation is well worthwhile. In the nineteenth and even in the early years of the twentieth centuries, parish records frequently referred to ceremonies taking place at church wells on special occasions, such as Easter Monday, Whit Sunday and more particularly on Trinity Sunday. Groups of boys and girls and young adults gathered at the church and together went to the appropriate wells, which very often had the same dedication as the churches they were associated with. Various small offerings were thrown into the water, of which the commonest were bent pins, before a ceremonial eating of cakes and drinking of sweetened water gave way to general dancing and merry-making. In the course of time, as the emphasis on enjoyment became ever stronger, the expedition came to resemble a Sunday School treat, whereas in fact it was the spiritual descendant of the ancient pilgrimage that took place from church to well on the patronal day. This patronal day custom too, be it remembered, was the successor in turn of the well-worship that was widespread in pre-Christian times when it was thought prudent to placate with suitable gifts the deities who were believed to live in wells.

Of the four wells to be visited two are in the north and two in the south. The first one is at Penmon in the south-east corner of Anglesey where Cynlas founded the first Christian church in the sixth century, appointing his brother Seiriol to be in charge. This first Christian church was destroyed by the Vikings in the tenth century, to be followed by the erection of the Norman church of today, less than a hundred yards north-east of which is St Seiriol's Well (G.R. 632808). The small rectangular room over the well was probably put up in the eighteenth century, underneath which is the well as Seiriol will have known it. Next to the well are the foundations of a hut, which in all probability was St Seiriol's cell.

Here the missionary lived and followed his calling, baptising in the well those he won over to Christianity. Just off the coast at this point is Puffin Island, which the Welsh call Ynys Seiriol, Seiriol's Island; on this little island are the remains of a monastery which in folk-memory is associated with St Seiriol. In the last chapter of this book a return visit will be made to Penmon in order to relate Penmon's reaction to Viking ruthlessness.

The most famous well in Wales is undoubtedly the one at Holywell *(Treffynnon)*, near the Dee Estuary. No further details need here be given about the legend that associated it with St Beuno and his courageous niece Winifred, whom he saved for higher things! Suffice it to say that St Winifred's Well, whether in origin pagan or Christian, has down the centuries attracted pilgrims who came there to take advantage of the water's healing powers. Beneath today's ornate church and well chamber is St Winifred's Well, in front of which is a bath where the afflicted seek relief from their ailments. Long before the Norman church was erected a cult had developed, partly as a result of the legend, and partly as a consequence of its growing reputation as a restorer of health. Its fame spread far and wide, and over the years three kings of England have gone there on pilgrimage, William the Conqueror, Edward the 1st and James the 2nd. The Catholic Church, in whose safe keeping the church and the well reside, treats the well as a Welsh Lourdes. As late as in the middle of the nineteenth century local records reported that large numbers of visitors came to the well every year. The immense flow of water was tapped early in the twentieth century by a local magnate who operated a lead mine but though the supply of water has in consequence been much reduced, its curative properties remain and the prosperity of the town of Holywell has therefore continued.

By way of a complete contrast the third well lies hidden in remote and hilly country, far beyond the reach of all but the totally committed for whom an appropriate reward will be forthcoming when finally they see Partrishow. The approach, preferably in a small car, is via the A465 Hereford to Abergavenny road. At Llanfihangel Crucornau turn north into the Honddu Valley as though going to Llanthony Abbey; after a mile and a half turn left at a telephone kiosk and continue on the narrow road for two miles until a crossroads is reached. The right-hand turning is labelled Partrishow but is better ignored as it involves half a mile of hard walking later on. Go on straight across the bridge and keep on this road to a T-junction, where the road to the right after a mile will lead to a really steep hill, at the foot of which is a flat place on the left hand side by a stream. Park here and cross the road to the well. This is the Holy Well of Issui, where the history of Partrishow began.

According to tradition, Issui, a sixth century Christian missionary, lived in a cell close to this well (G.R. 279224); from these modest headquarters he moved around the district, preaching, teaching and above all healing until one day a traveller, whom he had befriended, saw fit to murder him. Thereafter it was believed that the healing powers of Issui were transferred to his well, to which from then on pilgrimages were frequently made. This went on for many years until early in the eleventh century one of the pilgrims who had been smitten with leprosy, had the good fortune to be cured by the waters of the well, and in gratitude provided enough money for a church to be built up the hill above the well. This church, now called Partrishow, was at first known as Merthyr Issui, the Martyred Issui. A further reward will await today's visitors, who climb up the hill to the church, which is about a hundred yards above the well. They will find that magic has somehow survived at Partrishow.

The last well to be visited is near Tryleg, once a prosperous market town high up above the Wye valley, south of Monmouth in Gwent. Now called the Virtuous Well, because its chalybeate waters are believed to have cured many afflictions, it was in earlier times known as St Anne's Well. An early tradition asserted that there were at one time no fewer than nine wells in the neighbourhood, all of which were credited with curing different complaints.

EXTERNAL THREATS

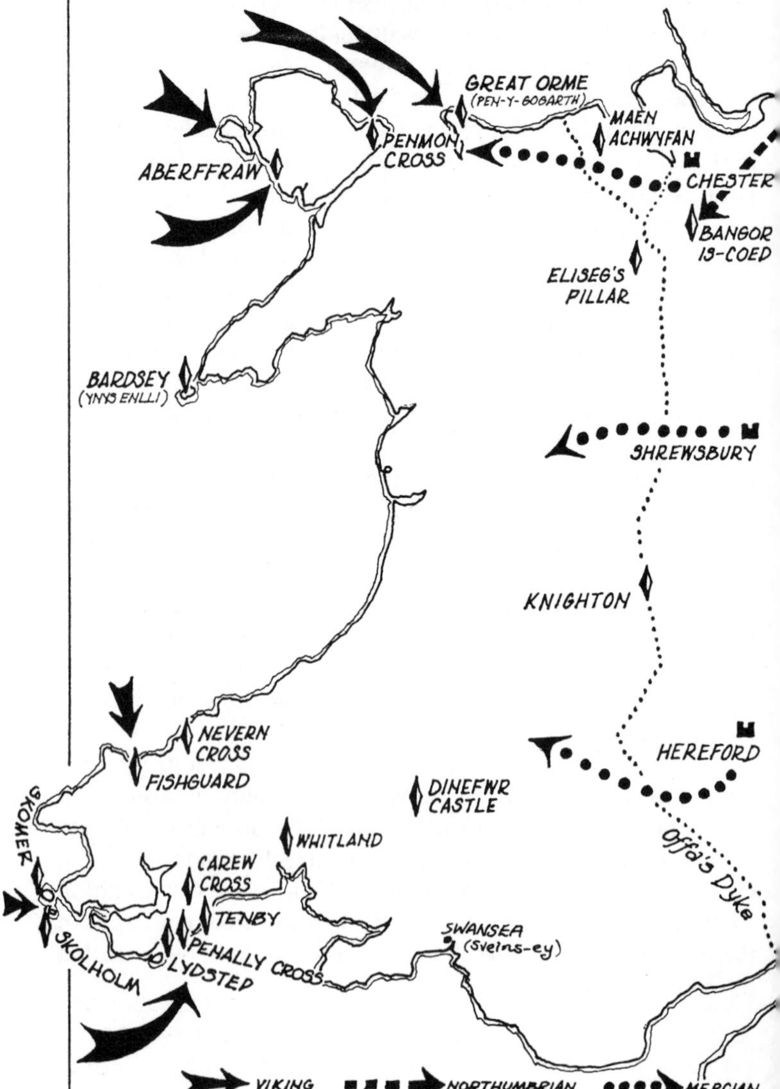

GREAT ORME
(PEN-Y-GOGARTH)

MAEN
ACHWYFAN

PENMON
CROSS

ABERFFRAW

CHESTER

BANGOR
IS-COED

ELISEG'S
PILLAR

BARDSEY
(YNYS ENLLI)

SHREWSBURY

KNIGHTON

HEREFORD

NEVERN
CROSS

FISHGUARD

DINEFWR
CASTLE

WHITLAND

CAREW
CROSS

TENBY

PENALLY CROSS

LYDSTEP

SWANSEA
(SVEINS-EY)

SKOMER

SKOLHOLM

Offa's Dyke

→ VIKING   ■ ■ ■▶ NORTHUMBRIAN   ●●●▶ MERCIAN

EXTERNAL THREATS

A. THE SAXON AND VIKING MENACE

Vacuum in Wales

Historians date the lapse of Roman power in Britain from 410 but in Wales the Roman writ ceased some years earlier, probably in 383, when the Emperor, the Spanish-born Christian soldier Magnus Maximus, whom the Welsh called Macsen Wledig when he married the Welsh Helen in Caernarfon, led away his Roman troops from Wales to undertake important new duties in distant Gaul. This Welsh wife was the same Helen whose name survives in the old Roman road, the Sarn Helen which still runs in a north-south direction here and there in Wales today. She has too sometimes been confused with the more famous Helen who was credited with having found the true cross when on a pilgrimage to Jerusalem; her even more famous son, the Emperor Constantine, has also sometimes been confused with the Welsh Helen's husband, the Emperor Magnus Maximus, despite the fact that Constantine ruled much earlier in the fourth century than the usurping Magnus Maximus. At any rate the vacuum, which Nature is believed to abhor, opened up in Wales after his departure from Caernarfon in 383.

Thereafter for a while there was no central authority in Wales, though at least in all probability it was spared the bitter turmoil that prevailed in areas further east in southern Britain after the withdrawal of the Roman legions. The invaluable evidence to be gathered from surviving inscribed Christian memorial stones in Wales in the fifth and sixth centuries suggests a society in which there was room for not only priests and missionaries but also for local government officers and even, as is proved by an inscription in a churchyard in the Llŷn Peninsula, for a doctor. However in southern parts of Wales the quarrels between evenly-matched, insecurely-organised and jealous Celtic tribes were of such a divisive nature that the clock was put back once the strong arm of Roman protection was lost. Another important factor operating in the south was the absence of the custom of primogeniture; estates became smaller as time went on and the laws of inheritance weakened the existing structure of local society. Thus the emergence of stronger units was thwarted, units which might have at least been able to assume some regional authority and exercise a measure of control over warring tribesmen.

In the course of this fifth century, when Wales for the most part lived a separate life untouched by the troubles that developed further east in Britain, early Saxon infiltration intensified, especially when the Anglo-Saxon leaders, Hengist and Horsa were invited to come to Britain by the Celtic leader Vortigern to help him defend his territories against Pictish assaults from the north. Vortigern, whose headquarters were probably in east Wales, and who, according to legend, married Hengist's daughter, played no proven part in Welsh events, despite the prominence assigned to him in folk-lore in connection with strange and magic happenings in the Gwynant Valley on Dinas Emrys, to which hill he possibly withdrew when the pressures of life elsewhere became too great for him to bear.

This same district around Snowdon is much concerned too with Arthurian legend; to the security of this mountainous area the wounded hero was carried, according to the legend, when his life was ebbing away. Arthur, about whose name much romantic nonsense crystallised in later days, more especially in the twelfth century, when Geoffrey of Monmouth embroidered and embellished the spoken tradition, seems to have been an outstanding Celtic leader in the first half of the sixth century, half a century after Vortigern had passed from the scene. To Arthur is given the credit for gaining a significant victory against the Saxons at Mount Badon in 516, the battle, Gildas assures his readers, having been fought on the very day of his birth, but where exactly it took place no-one seems to know.

The coming of Cunedda

At about this time when Wales was thus being cushioned from Saxon pressure, a new external threat developed in the north of the country, which began to fill the vacuum brought about by the retreat of Roman soldiers from Wales. As was briefly indicated in the last chapter, early in the fifth century Cunedda, a Romanised Celt, who was probably also a Christian, led his tribe of Votadini down from Strathclyde and managed to establish a foothold in the west of Anglesey, where from the headquarters he set up at Aberffraw he began to drive out the Irish immigrants from the island. His grandson Cadwallon completed the expulsion of the Irish from Anglesey when he defeated them in a battle fought near Trefdraeth in about 500. Cadwallon's son, Maelgwn Gwynedd went a step further, consolidating the political power of the family by centralising the government of north Wales and ruling it from Aberffraw. In the process he gave his name Gwynedd to the territory on the mainland that he had conquered. As the sixth century wore on, Cunedda's successors went from strength to strength until they ruled a domain that stretched from Anglesey in the north to the mouth of the river Teifi at Cardigan in the south.

Northumbrian invasion

Something has already been said about the historic and highly significant meetings that took place at Aust at the beginning of the seventh century, the effects of which were to widen the gap that already existed between the two branches of the Christian church in Britain. Sir Frank Stenton however, who is an outstanding authority on Anglo-Saxon England, sounded a note of caution. "An anecdote", he wrote, "never tells the whole truth about a complicated issue and there were many reasons besides Augustine's possible failure in courtesy for a breach between the Roman mission and the British church." Our knowledge of what happened in Britain in this seventh century suffers from overmuch reliance on the narratives of Bede, the only seventh-century chronicler of events and himself a Saxon with a thorough dislike of all things Celtic. The basic facts however are agreed. In the north-east Northumbria had begun to coalesce and to emerge as a force to be reckoned with. Under the leadership of Aethelfrith, their first able king, the boundaries of Northumbria were extended both northwards and to the west and south-west. Between 613 and 616 he attacked the Celts, whom we may now reasonably call the Welsh, on ground of his own choosing some miles to the south of Chester. Indeed it was from Aethelfrith's victory in this Battle of Chester that his fame as a successful leader was derived. The actual site of the battle was near the modern village of Bangor Is-coed (*Bangor-on-Dee*), the home of the great Celtic Christian monastery from whose much-respected precincts had gone forth those Christian emissaries who had done verbal battle with Augustine in the previous decade.

Tradition has it that before the fighting began a very large band of monks came out from the nearby monastery in order to pray for those who were about to defend themselves against the invading Aethelfrith and his men; the Northumbrian king, knowingly or otherwise proceeded to implement the terrible threat that Augustine had uttered at Aust. Aethelfrith slaughtered the monks to a man. The Welsh army, under the command of the son of the King of Powys, fared little better than the monks had done. The victorious Northumbrians, according to Giraldus Cambrensis, chose to celebrate by destroying Chester but developments elsewhere prevented Aethelfrith from following up his military success with territorial conquest. Nevertheless by this serious defeat the Welsh became geographically and politically isolated from their fellow Celts in Cumbria and Strathclyde.

Aethelfrith was succeeded as King of Northumbria by Edwin, who took upon himself the responsibility of continuing Northumbrian domination over the Celts by bringing about the complete destruction of the old northern kingdom of Elmet. It was this Edwin who managed to drive the final wedge between the Celts in the west and their fellows in the north. The tide eventually turned against him however when, after an attempt to capture parts of north Wales failed, he was thrown back and even pursued into his own territories by Cadwallon, scion of the house of Cunedda, who, in alliance with Northumbria's enemy Mercia, defeated and killed Edwin in 632. As things were to turn out this success of Cadwallon proved an illusion; his death in battle the following year near Hexham marked the end of the very last attempt on the part of the Western Celts to win back any of the lands in the east which their forebears had formerly inhabited.

By the year 650 the Welsh seem to have accepted the geographical boundaries of contemporary Wales as the limit of their homeland for the foreseeable future. The resulting isolation, which was to continue for about a hundred years, was rendered the more necessary by the stark fact that the men of Mercia (the Mercian-Welsh alliance having proved to be of very short duration) now firmly controlled Herefordshire and Shropshire. From the middle of the seventh to the middle of the eighth century the Welsh turned in upon themselves; consciously or unconsciously in those years of separation they went on the defensive. They became introspective, as they developed their own language, their own culture, their own institutions, their own self-consciousness.

The centre of government and administration was at Aberffraw, the strong-hold established earlier in the west of Anglesey by Cunedda, and faithfully handed down to his successors. In the nearby settlement of Llangadwaladr may still be seen in the parish church historical evidence of events of the early seventh century. In the chancel stands the so-called Catamanus Stone, which was erected to the memory of Cadfan, who died in 625. As well as being a famous king, as the inscription asserted, he was also a famous father as his son was none other than that Cadwallon, who had encompassed the defeat of Edwin of Northumbria.

Mercian aggression

The years of introspection were savagely swept away by the aggressive intentions of the Anglo-Saxons of Mercia; it was in the eighth century that two rulers of Mercia, first Aethelbald and then Offa, fortified their western frontiers with the Welsh. The earlier of the two defence systems, Wat's Dyke, was erected to secure the northern end of Mercia's boundary with Wales, its builders presumably taking advantage of the Roman road system, based on Chester, in order to bring up supplies for the vital work of construction. Here, near Basingwerk, on the Dee estuary there is still impressive evidence of the first man-made boundary between the Saxons and the Welsh.

Offa ruled Mercia from 757 to 796; though his reign was for the most part a very turbulent one, it seems likely that the great earthwork associated with his name was thrown up in a period of relative peace, probably between 784 and 795, when it is known that an uneasy peace prevailed along the frontier. Offa's Dyke, which marked a more or less continuous barrier from the Severn valley in the south to the estuary of the Dee in the north, not only spelt out to the Welsh, "Thus far and no further", but at the same time signified a tacit Mercian acceptance of the Welsh right to rule themselves and may be seen as proof positive of the sterling qualities of leadership shown by the Welsh, more particularly by the princes of Powys. To thoughtful observers Offa's Dyke and the surviving portions of Wat's Dyke provide eloquent twentieth century witness of those troubled years. In addition attention must be drawn to what is probably the most famous memorial in the whole of Wales, Eliseg's Pillar, which stands in a field near Valle Crucis Abbey to the north of Llangollen. Details of this will be given in the next chapter.

The respite in Mercian-Welsh warfare came to an abrupt end in 796, when Offa once again, though for the last time, took the offensive. This attack was followed by a number of others, mounted by his successors in the early years of the ninth century. In 816 Cenwulf invaded the north and managed to get as far as the Snowdonia region; two years later he turned his attention to Dyfed in the south. When in 821 he died at Basingwerk, he was on the eve of launching yet another campaign against the Welsh. The very next year the new king of Mercia, Ceowulf, the brother of Cenwulf, captured Deganwy before turning south and overrunning Powys. These bitter incursions between 816 and 822 that seemed to represent a new phase in the Mercian attempt to impose its authority over Wales, in fact came to an unexpected end when the Mercians found themselves threatened by a new and formidable enemy from the east, the Vikings. Thereafter the kingdom of Mercia quite swiftly fell into a decline as the Viking power gathered strength, to the immediate discomfiture of all Saxons and Welshmen alike.

The arrival of the Vikings

These new disturbers of the peace came from the northern lands. Northmen or Norsemen, Vikings or Danes, whatever name was given to them, they showed themselves to be restless travellers and ruthless fighters. Those who concentrated on attacks from the sea proved themselves such skilful navigators that their expeditions took them to Spain and to Italy, to Iceland and to Russia, to France and to various parts of the British Isles. When Charlemagne, who had established in western Europe an empire based on Christian law and order died in 814, his dominions soon crumbled. The men from the north saw their chance and took it. Everywhere they went, their impact was immense; nowhere was it stronger than in Ireland, where an Irish golden age suddenly collapsed in 853, when the Vikings made themselves lords of that island. Their overlordship there was to last for a century and a half and, while it lasted, Wales was made to feel the full blast of Viking attacks, which were mounted from Irish bases.

The very year of this Irish disaster saw the first Viking raid on Anglesey; thereafter the Vikings harried the coasts of Wales, north and south, on and off for the hundred and fifty years of their Irish occupation. Anglesey itself was invaded on no fewer than seven occasions, the last being in 987. Last of all the Viking incursions into Wales was made in 999, when St David's was devastated, and its bishop murdered. Monasteries and churches were looted and laid waste in those widespread raids, in the course of which a number of Viking trading stations were established along the coasts of Wales. Many a place name on Welsh coast and island bears witness to those terrible times when the Viking writ for the time being ran. Tenby *(Dinbych-y-pysgod)*, Bardsey *(Enlli)*, the Great Orme, Fishguard, Lydstep, Skolholm and Skomer all speak of their Viking past.

Rhodri Mawr

It was in this tragic period of Welsh history, when the Vikings were attacking from the sea that her south-eastern neighbours, Wessex, were being similarly threatened by other would-be conquerors from the north, the Danes. Just as the dire emergency produced the right leader in Wessex in the person of Alfred the Great, so too in Wales it threw up the mighty Rhodri Mawr, Rhodri the Great. During the first half of the ninth century the course of Welsh history changed direction as the ruling house of Gwynedd set about trying to unify the country, the process seeming to start with Merfyn Frych, the King of Gwynedd, seeking a dynastic marriage. In this, the generation before the Viking threat developed, the well-being of Wales was still being menaced by repeated Mercian thrusts. In order to strengthen Welsh resistance to these attacks, most of which were directed at Powys, Merfyn married Nest, the sister of Powys' resourceful king, Cyngen, and thereby secured an immediate and valuable ally.

When Merfyn died in 844, he was able to bequeath to his son, Rhodri both Gwynedd and Powys; to this inheritance Rhodri later added other parts of central and south Wales with the result that in the course of his thirty-four years' reign he became master of all north and central Wales and a very large part of south Wales too. Like his father before him, he had made a politically wise marriage when he joined forces with Angharad, the sister of the last king of Cardigan, who in his lifetime had taken over Carmarthen, forming out of the two areas the new kingdom of Seisyllwg.

Thus strengthened at home, Rhodri felt strong enough to face up to the daunting task of trying to hold at bay the Vikings, whose first main target was Anglesey, where in 854 he defeated and killed the Viking leader, Gorm. The respite gained was short-lived, however; nevertheless, while throughout his reign he was plagued by repeated Viking attacks, which he could do nothing to prevent, he at least made sure that these raids could not be followed up by territorial conquest and settlement. On a hill outside Llandeilo, in the Towy Valley in Dyfed, stands the casetle of Dinefwr. Here in 876, two years before he died, Rhodri made the necessary arrangements for the future government of Wales after his death. In order to give Wales the unity which he believed she desperately needed he agreed to divide his dominions into three parts, to be inherited by the three strongest of his six sons, one to succeed him in the north, another in the centre and the third in the south.

Not all the rulers who have acquired the designation of "Great" have really merited the honour; in the case of Rhodri it is perhaps easier than usual to justify the accompanying 'Mawr'. His achievement in dealing so firmly with the enemy at the gate was simple and perhaps negative, but he did at least reduce the Viking menace to manageable proportions, while his court achieved the reputation of being a civilised place where foreigners were free to come and go and where they could speak their own tongues and be understood. Rhodri certainly showed real foresight in planning for future Welsh unity and although those who came after him failed to unify their country, he had provided them with a dynasty which was to rule Wales, both north and south, for many a long year.

By way of footnote it should be added that the young Saxon Alfred, who was also to be known as the Great, had by this time become the King of Wessex and it is perhaps significant that a year or two after Rhodri's death in 878 his son, Anarawd, who had inherited Gwynedd, saw fit to pay allegiance to Alfred, becoming the first Welshman ever to visit a Saxon court. It has to be borne in mind however, that towards the end of the ninth century the Viking menace had become so fearsome throughout Western Europe that Alfred's success in dealing with the Danes had caused him to be venerated as the great Christian champion against what were seen as the marauding heathens from the north.

Hywel Dda

Hywel Dda, a grandson of Rhodri Mawr, became ruler of Seisyllwg in 910, at a time when Gwynedd and Powys had once again good reason to fear a renewal of aggression on the part of Mercia. In 911 Aethelflaeda, the daughter of Alfred the Great and sister of Edward the Elder, the King of Wessex, herself became ruler of Mercia, when her husband Aethelred died. For the following eight years there was real anxiety west of Offa's Dyke as the "Lady of the Mercians" proceeded to fortify strong points at Runcorn in the north on the invasion route into Gwynedd and at Chirbury on the well-worn way into central Wales. Having thus secured herself, she took the initiative and in 916, as the Anglo-Saxon Chronicle records, sent her army into Powys; in the course of this aggressive campaign the Mercian army destroyed a Welsh stronghold, which had been built in the middle of Llan-gors Lake on an artificially-created island, a stronghold, which underwater archaeologists in the summer of 1988 uncovered, dating its building to about 870. Indeed the new threat implicit in the renewal of Mercian ambitions must have been an important factor in the gradual development of an understanding between the various princes of Wales and Wessex. In addition it is known that Hywel had in his early years greatly admired the achievements of Alfred the Great, especially his stalwart defence of his lands against the Danes. From about 918 the understanding between Welshmen and the men of Wessex flourished and grew into a special relationship between Hywel and Alfred's son, Edward the Elder, ruler of Wessex from 910 to 925, who for his part had earned deep Welsh gratitude for securing the release from the Vikings of the Bishop of Llandaf, who had been carried off in a raid.

Hywel Dda had followed in the footsteps of his famous grandfather and great grandfather by greatly increasing his dominions as a result of making a successful marriage. His wife, Elen, daughter of the King of Pembroke, was to bring her husband all the lands south-west of Seisyllwg. Again, when Hywel's cousin, Idwal, the King of Gwynedd, and another grandson of Rhodri died, Hywel was able without much effort and without attracting too much attention to take over both Gwynedd and Powys. Thus Hywel found himself, halfway through his reign, virtual ruler of all Wales, enabling him, when he went on pilgrimage to Rome in 928, to be thought of as, "the King of all the Welsh."

Clearly in the reign of Hywel Dda the centre of Welsh political gravity moved for the first time since the days of Cunedda from the north of the country to the south. At the same time as this geographical shift of power occurred there came an equally significant shift in policy as the ruler of Wales moved from hostility towards Saxons to co-operation with them. This was no easy change of attitude nor did it go unchallenged, though the challenge failed. Further evidence of this desire to co-operate with Wessex came in the reign of Athelstan, who succeeded his father Edward on the throne of Wessex in 925. Between then and 928 representatives from Wales met the new King of Wessex in Hereford. At this meeting it became clear that Welshmen even admitted the overlordship of their host, to whom they swore allegiance. The ever-present Viking threat all along the coasts of Wales may well have been the determining factor that made the Welsh accept dependence as the price they were prepared to pay to acquire a friend and ally in the emergency; if the understanding did in fact amount to an alliance, then the Welsh were definitely the junior partners. A limited territorial arrangement agreed upon at Hereford concerned the mutual recognition in that area of the river Wye as the boundary between Welsh and Saxon lands.

Protected by this understanding with Wessex and politically strengthened by it, Hywel ordered the leading Welsh clergy and the most important laymen to meet him at Whitland

(Hendy-gwyn) in 930. There, a few miles west of Carmarthen, he presented for their earnest consideration and discussion the whole corpus of Welsh law and custom. That they were entrusted with the responsibility of reforming and categorising Welsh laws in this authoritative fashion is proof positive of the powerful position enjoyed by Hywel Dda. This assembly stayed in continual session for forty days, by which time the all-important decisions had all been taken. For just how much of this codification Hywel was personally responsible cannot now be known for certain and indeed is sometimes disputed but his title of Dda dates from this time. Few kings in history have gained the description of Good but Hywel by his legal work and his persistent attempt to reconcile the religious differences between the Celtic church and Rome seems to have justified the title, especially when it be remembered that throughout his reign the Vikings posed an ever-present threat. It is worth recalling that, when in after years Edward I of England in 1284 saw fit at Rhuddlan to dictate terms to the Welsh, he thought he was softening the blow by suggesting that he had only based his statute on the laws coded by Hywel. That Hywel Dda was a wise and diplomatic ruler cannot be denied nor should the years of peace that his policies made possible with his neighbours be underrated. Whether he was good and not just opportunist may be argued, though the laws associated with his name have stood the test of time. Unhappily peace seems to have died with him in 950.

All the efforts of Rhodri Mawr to create Welsh unity by providing the country with a strong dynasty seemed to have failed in the very dark years that followed the death of his grandson Hywel Dda in 950. Hywel for his part had shown one way to peace and unity by co-operating with the Saxons of Wessex; that policy too came to an abrupt end. Even the unifying effect on the Welsh of the constant threat of Viking raids lost its former power, despite the stark fact that half a century more of these ferocious attacks had still to be endured in Wales. The lack of any strong central government showed itself too in the excessive power still being enjoyed at the local level by regional princelings; in fact much of Wales was still a simple society where allegiance to the local family was paramount. All these facts, in addition to the ancient practice of dividing a man's lands between all his sons when he died, together presented Wales with an acute crisis in the middle years of the tenth century, when they suddenly lost the authority of Hywel Dda. This unhappy situation was to become the more serious in the years that followed because their adversaries across Offa's Dyke were beginning to take big steps towards achieving their own national unity.

Hence the pattern of events was extremely confused in the second half of the tenth century, as the various descendants of Hywel Dda in different parts of the country indulged in fratricidal contention with each other. In those uncertain times no prince in the north, in the centre or in the south, was strong enough to gain the mastery, which would have enabled him at least for the time being once again to have achieved the unification of Wales, as Rhodri Mawr and Hywel Dda had done in the past. In 986 a glimmer of hope had appeared but it was to be snuffed out before the end of the century. Hywel Dda's grandson, Maredudd ab Owain in 986 held sway in Gwynedd, Deheubarth and in Dyfed but failed to annex Powys. In 992 he found himself at war with his own nephew, who proceeded to bring in to help him against his uncle an army from Mercia. Maredudd died in 999 and the new century dawned on a Wales more divided than ever.

Gruffudd ap Llywelyn and Saxon Harold

Those very dark hours for Welsh hopes preceded a dawn which lit up the personality of one of the greatest of all Welsh military leaders, Gruffudd ap Llywelyn, whose father Llywelyn ap Seisyll had seized the throne of Gwynedd in 1018, a domain which he was to rule successfully until 1023. His son, Gruffudd, according to surviving records, was indolent in his youth, reserving his appearance in public life until 1037 when the King of Gwynedd was cut down by his own men. In the aftermath of this murder, in which Gruffudd himself may well have played a part, he began to stand out as the strong man whom Wales had been looking for. He became King of Gwynedd in 1039, adding Powys to his dominions later in the same year. Before long he had in addition annexed Deheubarth, Mornanwg (modern Glamorgan) and Gwent. In fact he was thereafter virtually the ruler of all Wales for the rest of his reign.

Gruffudd was a man of immense physical energy and courage: he not only unified Wales (killing many Welshmen in the process) but took the offensive against the English, making a number of successful forays across Offa's Dyke. In 1052 he won a battle near Leominster, following it up three years later by killing five hundred English soldiers in the course of capturing Hereford, where, if the local reports are to be believed, seven cathedral canons stoutly defended the great west door of their church before it was battered down by Gruffudd's men. In 1056 he crossed the dyke once more and again captured Hereford before English reinforcements made him withdraw into the Welsh hills.

Gruffudd's reign roughly coincided with that of the English king, Edward the Confessor, whose right-hand man was the Saxon leader, Harold, Earl of Hereford, destined on Edward's death to become the last Saxon king of England. These two giants of men, Gruffudd and Harold were worthy adversaries; it is perhaps ironical that it was in the reign of one of Wales' strongest and most successful rulers that the hated Saxons came nearest to establishing themselves in Wales. Harold managed to set up Saxon strongholds in Gwent and Powys before setting forth on the invasion of North Wales which he attempted in 1062 and 1063. Apparently Harold alone of those who sought to impose their wills upon Wales had given the necessary thought to the choice of suitable tactics. Giraldus Cambrensis, writing a hundred years later, spoke highly of his skill as a military planner. He wrote: "He advanced into Wales on foot, at the head of his lightly-clad infantry, lived on the country and marched up and down and round and about the whole of Wales." At any rate in 1063 he drove Gruffudd out of his castle at Rhuddlan before destroying it, and then systematically approached the mountainous area around Snowdon, supported by a fleet that stood off the Welsh coast to prevent Gruffudd from receiving supplies from Anglesey. By the end of that tragic summer Gruffudd was on the run; he was to be hunted down and eventually killed by his own Welsh supporters. The despatch of his severed head to Harold marked the end of hostilities and the temporary recognition of the Saxon subjection of North Wales.

Harold's victory was however of short duration: three years later he died in a hail of arrows at Hastings, thereafter leaving Wales exposed to a greater threat even than that ever presented by the Saxons. Gruffudd, despite his humiliating failure in 1063, had by his bravery and leadership stiffened Welsh resolve to resist further invasion. When the Normans, after their rapid conquest and assimilation of England, turned westwards to deal with Wales, they were to be made aware of the strength of Welsh national feeling, which Gruffudd had by his example greatly fostered in his fellow countrymen. The Earls of Hereford, Shrewsbury and Chester, specially created by the Conqueror to extend his authority to the west of Offa's Dyke, were soon to realise the severity of the task assigned to them.

Maen Achwyfan (Whitford Cross): Maen Achwyfan stands in the corner of a field, one mile west of the village of Whitford, which is three miles N.W. of Holywell in Clwyd. This disc-headed monument, the tallest Celtic cross outside Scotland, was put up at the end of the tenth century; all its surfaces are covered with complicated Celtic and Scandinavian designs but the ravages of time have made many of the shapes hard to identify.

B. EVIDENCE IN WALES TODAY

Modern wars leave in their wake destruction and war memorials whereas the periodical blood-letting that Saxons and Vikings inflicted on the Welsh left few traces of their activities that were discernible to succeeding generations. Hence surviving evidence of the tumultuous times described in the last chapter is very thin indeed; the backward looking enquirer today, who has already been well rewarded by the sight of barrows, long and round, iron-age camps, Roman remains and Christian memorial stones, will now have to be content with a few, though wonderful crosses and with Mercian Offa's attempt to bring about a permanent line of demarcation between his domains and those of the Welsh, whose independence was being recognised by the erection of this dyke.

Two miles north of Llangollen are the spectacular ruins of the Cistercian Valle Crucis Abbey, in a field not far from which stands what is probably the most famous memorial in Wales, Eliseg's Pillar (G.R. 203445). Originally it was about twice its present height, having in its long history lost both its cross-head and the lower part of its shaft. The cross was sufficiently prominent in the twelfth century for the Cistercian monks who were engaged in building nearby to name their abbey after the cross which they saw every time they looked up from their work. It was erected early in the ninth century by a king of Powys, Cyngen (who died in Rome in 854) to commemorate the life and martial achievements of his great grandfather, Elise, who was the contemporary of Offa and a worthy opponent of the much-dreaded king of Mercia. The monument was eight hundred years old when disaster struck; in the course of the civil wars in the seventeenth century fanatical Puritans hacked at

Nevern Cross: Erected in the churchyard in c. 1000 A.D., it is similar in appearance to those at Whitford and Carew. This splendid Celtic monument, about 13 feet high, thanks to the protection afforded by its proximity to the church, has suffered less than most crosses from the passage of the years.

it with venomous fury, seeing in it some reminder of 'Popish practices'. Fortunately for posterity a complete transcript of the inscription on the pillar had been made in the previous century. The pillar lay in ruins until towards the end of the eighteenth century that part that had survived was put together and re-erected in its present position on a low mound, which is thought by some to have been the site of a Christian burial in the fifth or early sixth century.

Eliseg's Pillar must have been one of the first of the free-standing crosses as there is no record of one being erected before the ninth century. The other crosses that have survived mostly date from the early tenth century or later; of these those in the north are thought to have been carved by Celtic craftsmen who had been forced by Viking raiders to leave their homes in Northumbria and in Ireland before taking refuge in North Wales. Their crosses are noted for the scenes they portray, both human and animal, whereas those in the south of the country were probably the work of local craftsmen who for the most part concentrated on complicated geometrical patterns.

Three of these southern crosses with similar, though by no means identical, motifs will be described, the first at Penally, south of Tenby, not far from Manorbier Castle in south Dyfed. St Teilo, the friend and contemporary of St David, is believed to have been both born and buried in Penally (G.R. 118992), in whose churchyard there used to stand a tall and beautifully-carved Celtic cross. Today it adorns the south transept of the church near the remains of another early cross, also brought indoors from the churchyard; this one, which unfortunately has lost its cross, dates from the end of the ninth century, while the other one was probably put up a few years later.

A few miles to the north-west of Penally *(Panalun)*, Carew Cross *(Caeriw)* (G.R. 047037) rises majestically at the side of the A4075, about equidistant between Pembroke and Tenby; behind it loom the spectacular ruins of Carew Castle, one of the most impressive castles in South Wales, but several centuries younger than the cross, which at nearly fourteen feet is one of the tallest Celtic crosses in Wales as well as being one of the most

Carew Cross: Carew is in south Dyfed, halfway between Pembroke and Tenby. This intricately-carved early Christian cross, 14 feet high, probably dates from the 9th century; it stands high up above the main road, with the spectacular ruins of Carew Castle acting as a backcloth. The commemorative panel near the base bears witness to a later event.

132

intricately-carved, with complicated patterns on both sides and faces of the shaft. A memorial tablet commemorates one Maredudd, son of Edwin, a Welsh prince who was killed in battle in 1035. It is possible however that this commemorative tablet to the prince was added many years after the cross was erected, which could well have been in the ninth century.

A second visit to Nevern church is necessary in order to wonder at the free-standing cross which dominates the south side of the churchyard. Thought to have been erected in about 1000, the cross is reminiscent of the one just seen at Carew and the one still to be looked at at Whitford *(Maen Achwyfan)*. It is about thirteen feet high, with the surfaces on all four sides of the shaft and the cross-head covered with interlaced decorations of a geometric type. The inscriptions on both faces of the shaft have so far defeated all attempts at deciphering.

Before leaving the south a short visit is recommended to the church at Llanilltud Fawr, wherein will be found the remains of several crosses, dating from the ninth or early tenth centuries, in addition to a ninth century cross with a Latin inscription to Samson, who may have been an abbot in the local monastery.

To see the last two crosses a return has to be made to the north. One is in Anglesey, the other in eastern Clwyd, not far from the Dee estuary. This latter one may be visited at the same time as St Winifred's Well in Holywell, as the cross at Whitford (Maen Achwyfan) which is over eleven feet high stands in a corner of a field, a mile west of the village of Whitford *(Chwitffordd)*. Dating from the tenth or the eleventh century this wheel cross (G.R. 129787) is carved on all surfaces, its rich decoration an interesting mixture of Scandinavian and Celtic influences. The passage of the years has unfortunately been unkind to this monument, some of its motifs no longer being recognisable.

The last of a number of visits to Anglesey concerns two crosses at Penmon, which has already been described in connection with St Seiriol's Well. The Vikings, whose raids on Wales from newly-acquired bases in Ireland, bedevilled life in Wales for so many years, first attacked Anglesey in 844, before returning to ravage Penmon in 971. The well-known but now miscalled Deer Park Cross was erected in about 1000, to take the place of an

Eliseg's Pillar: 2 miles north of Llangollen in Clwyd, in a field near the ruins of the Cistercian abbey, Valle Crucis. Truncated and defaced by religious fanaticism in later centuries, today's monument is only about half its original height, having lost its cross and part of its shaft. Erected in the early 9th century, it was probably the first cross to be put up in Wales. Refer back to the text for the details of this, the most famous early monument in Wales.

earlier one, destroyed by the Vikings thirty years previously. This outstanding monument, now in a new position in the nave of the church, consists of a shaft, crowned by a circular head, from which stone arms extend on both sides to complete the cross. The decoration, as in all the Celtic crosses seen, is elaborate and intricate, but this one at Penmon has in addition sculptures of human beings and animals; the Celtic tradition here has been reinforced by Scandinavian and Irish influences. There is another tall cross in the church, believed also to date from about 1000; this one stands in the south transept.

The last area to be recommended in this book is Offa's Dyke, the exploration of which affords satisfaction to historians, walkers and nature-lovers alike. In 1971 the Offa's Dyke Long Distance Footpath came into existence; this path, which links Prestatyn with Chepstow, is a hundred and sixty eight miles long and incorporates in it sixty good miles of surviving and recognisable dyke. The Offa's Dyke Association, which looks after the welfare of the dyke and of those who choose to walk upon it, has its headquarters in Knighton, whose Welsh name proclaims its geographical situation, Trefyclo, the Town on the Dyke. Those who want to get a feel of the dyke without involving themselves in too much exercise, can do so both north and south of Knighton, leaving their cars in the town and first paying a visit to the old Primary school, under whose roof will be found the hospitable office of the Offa's Dyke Association, an admirable exhibition of life in these Marches in former times, and a Youth Hostel. That the dyke rises both north and south of Knighton illustrates an important fact, namely that it was not intended to be a barrier to keep the Welsh out of Mercia or the men of Mercia out of Wales, but rather it was an attempt to control the passage of men and goods from Mercia into Wales and from Wales to Mercia. The presence of this and other gaps in the dyke was to ensure the proper regulation of movement in both directions.

One particular central section of the dyke has been selected for a closer view to show the impact that it must have made on the ordering of social life in the Marches, the section between the Kerry Ridgeway, west of Bishop's Castle and Churchtown,

A section of Offa's Dyke.

further south. This area lies inside the mountainous middle section between Montgomery and Knighton. (The B4386 from Montgomery, eastwards towards Chirbury, crosses the dyke a mile east of the town at a point where the dyke is still the national frontier). Those wanting to get the most enjoyment out of exploring the walk about to be described need a car and a considerate driver who will be prepared to drop them at the Kerry Ridgeway (G.R. 258896) and pick them up later at Churchtown (G.R. 263873). It is suggested that the approach by car should be made from Bishop's Castle, a busy little market town in west Shropshire. Take the ever-narrowing country road due west of the parish church which is at the bottom of the main street, and continue on it for about three miles until Bishopsmoat is reached, noting in the field on the right a well-preserved Norman motte and bailey. At the intersection of roads take the middle one, labelled Pantglas; another cross-roads is approached after about a mile and a half at Hazel Bank, with a telephone kiosk at the lefthand side. One mile further on is the Kerry Ridgeway, where an Offa's Dyke fingerpost, decorated with an acorn, will be seen on a stile on the left bank. Here the walk begins. The car driver, if wise, will retrace his steps to Bishop's Castle, where he should turn south on to the A488. About two and a half miles along this road turn right onto another country road, marked Cefn Einion, from where he should use his Ordnance Survey map to get to Churchtown for the eventual rendezvous with his passengers.

The walkers meanwhile will have climbed up the bank on to the dyke itself, which on the Kerry Ridgeway is thirteen hundred feet above sea level. The path soon leads over a stile into a waymarked wood at the bottom of which is the little river Unk, which has to be crossed by a wooden plank. Ahead rises the dyke again which now leads steeply to a narrow road, which crosses it on Edenhope Hill (G.R. 263883). When some breath has been regained and the spectacular views absorbed, cross the road and get back on to the dyke which stays on the level for about a third of a mile until it crosses a lane, running at right angles over it, when it drops down sharply into the next valley at Churchtown which today consists of a house or two and the parish church of

Mainstone, (the hamlet of that name lying a mile further to the east). This church has the distinction of being the only Anglican church in Shropshire not to be mentioned by Pevsner! It is probable that a little community grew up here in early times to satisfy the needs of those who passed that way through the gap in the dyke. Before getting back to the waiting car, cast a glance across the road to where the dyke soon climbs steeply up again and out of sight on to wild and beautiful country to the west of Clun.

BIBLIOGRAPHY

Bowen, E.G.,*The Settlements of the Celtic Saints of Wales.*
Giraldus Cambrensis, *Itinerary of Wales.*
Houlder, C., *Wales: An Archaeological Guide.*
Jones, Francis, *The Holy Wells of Wales.*
Nash-Williams, V.E., *The Early Christian Monuments of Wales.*
Wheeler, R.E.M., *Prehistoric and Roman Wales.*
Williams, A.H., *An Introduction to the History of Wales,* Vol. I
Prehistoric Times to AD 1063.

ACKNOWLEDGEMENTS

The following are the owners of the copyright of the illustrations
and have kindly permitted their use.

NATIONAL MUSEUM OF WALES
(on pages 42(a), 56, 84(a), 96(a) and (b), 102 and 128)

ROYAL COMMISSION ON ANCIENT AND HISTORICAL MONUMENTS IN WALES
(CROWN COPYRIGHT)
(on pages 28(b), 30(a), 32(b), 42(b), 58(b), 64, 84, 98, 104, 130 and 132)

GWASG CARREG GWALCH
(on pages 28(a), 44(a) and (b))

PETER HAVILAND, FALCON STUDIOS, PENMACHNO
(on pages 86, 88, 91 and 92)

The rest of the photographs were taken by my wife and are her
copyright.

INDEX OF PLACE NAMES